Daylight at Midnight

D0512992

Daylight at Midnight

Reflections for Women on the Book of Esther

Jane McNabb

Authentic

MILTON KEYNES ● COLORADO SPRINGS ● HYDERABAD

First published 2007 by Authentic Media
9 Holdom Avenue, Bletchley, Milton Keynes, Bucks, MK1 1QR, UK
1820 Jet Stream Drive, Colorado Springs, CO 80921, USA
OM Authentic Media, Medchal Road, Jeedimetla Village,
Secunderabad 500 055, A.P., India
www.authenticmedia.co.uk
Authentic Media is a division of IBS-STL U.K., limited by guarantee, with its
Registered Office at Kingstown Broadway, Carlisle, Cumbria CA3 0HA.
Registered in England & Wales No. 1216232. Registered charity 270162

British Library Cataloguing in Publication Data
A catalogue record for this book is available from the
British Library
ISBN-13: 978-1-85078-756-3

Design by James Kessell for Scratch the Sky Ltd.
(www.scratchthesky.com)
Print Management by Adare Carwin
Printed in Great Britain by J.H. Haynes & Co., Sparkford

In memory of Rene Chapman who, by example,
taught me to look for God's daylight at midnight

Contents

Contents

Timeline

568BC	Nebuchadnezzar, King of Babylon, sacks Jerusalem.
539BC	Babylon falls to Cyrus, King of Mede-Persia. Many Jews relocated throughout new empire.
538BC	First return of Jews to Jerusalem. Ezra 1–6.
486BC	Xerxes becomes King of Persia, succeeding Darius I.
483BC	Account of Esther begins in Esther 1.
481–479BC	Failed war with Greece.
490BC	Esther prepared. Esther 2:12.
479BC	War with Greece ends. Revolt in Babylon. Esther taken to the king. Esther 2: 16.
473BC	Account of Esther ends.
465BC	Xerxes assassinated.
458BC	Second return of the Jews. Ezra 7–10.
445BC	Third return of the Jews. Nehemiah 1–2.

Introduction

'Where are you God?' is a question that most of us ask at some point in our lives. Perhaps even at this moment your faith is more than a little shaky – the past haunts you, the present is crushing you and fears for the future are threatening to overwhelm you.

If you, like me, need hope, join me in this look at Esther. She had every reason to feel as we do, and probably more. As well as her own problems she carried the weight of an entire nation on her shoulders.

Her society wasn't so different from ours. Headlines of her day would transfer quite easily into our newspapers – the conflict between superpowers, political intrigue and corruption, the consequences of immorality and the widespread persecution of God's people.

Esther's life, which on the surface appears dreamlike and glamorous – the ideal Cinderella story – in reality was far from such. She knew heartache and pain just like us. I wonder if she asked 'Where are you God?'

This is the only book in the Bible where God isn't actually mentioned by name and yet it's filled to overflowing with his presence and constantly moves to the sound of his voice. The time scan of the story cannot contain him. He enters the scene from the past and exits to the future.

He works *for* his people and *through* his people even in the most hideous of circumstances.

Esther's story is about deliverance of a woman, a nation and ultimately of a world. It tells of the escape from fear and death. But it's about more than that. It's about hope and life.

At the Jews' lowest point, not long after their exile into Babylon and 85 years before the account in Esther begins, a letter arrived addressed to them. The hand was Jeremiah's but the words were God's. 'I know the plans I have for you . . . They are plans for good and not for disaster, to give you a future and a hope.' (Jer. 29:11)

God not only promises deliverance but also a reason to live. Esther was part of this future, this plan and this hope.

Johanna-Ruth Dobschiner was a Jewess who miraculously survived World War Two while her entire family perished in concentration camps. During this time she met with Jesus Christ. He changed her life. Her thrilling autobiography has become a Christian classic and is entitled *Selected to Live*.

She writes:

> I am puzzled and bewildered by the experience which war and deprivation pressed on us all, but have learned that a loving, invisible hand held mine through it all and I am firmly convinced that neither death nor life, nor angels, nor principalities, nor things present, nor things to come, will be able to separate me from the love of God, which is revealed in Christ Jesus.[1]

We too have been selected. Selected to meet him, to know him, to experience him and to love him. He has selected us to live.

1

Persians, Parties and Power

☞ *Read ESTHER 1*

On 21 May 2006, England's captain David Beckham and wife Victoria threw a star-studded farewell party for the World Cup team.

The mean and moody line-up of players was in black tie, accompanied by their wives or girlfriends in glamorous designer-label gowns. Victoria was resplendent in two million pounds' worth of Asprey diamonds and a yellow gown that complemented a towering arrangement of sunflowers and lemons piled underneath four orange trees, specially flown in from Seville. The party was held in a marquee the size of a football pitch on the lawn outside their Hertfordshire home. Guests dined on Gordon Ramsay cuisine at tables surmounted by birch trees decorated with silk butterflies and planted in white rose and tulip beds. After a charity auction, where almost the price of Victoria's outfit was raised, entertainment was supplied by Robbie Williams and the late 'Godfather of Soul', James Brown.

Defeat was far from everyone's mind that night. If only the play during the following weeks had matched the flamboyance of the occasion that preceded it.

The Book of Esther opens with King Xerxes throwing an even more impressive party, one that would never be forgotten.

Date: 483BC

Party Number 1

> In the third year of his reign, he [King Xerxes] gave a banquet for all his princes and officials. He invited all the military officers of Media and Persia, as well as the noblemen and provincial officials. The celebration lasted six months—a tremendous display of the opulent wealth and glory of his empire. (Esth. 1:3–4)

Three years into his reign, this banquet was both a mark of kindness to those who served him loyally and an unabashed display of human greatness and opulence. Perhaps too, this was another send-off party, not for a football tournament but a far greater conflict – the planned war with the Greeks, a war Xerxes fully expected to win.

Although Xerxes wasn't the oldest of the royal half-brothers, his mother Atossa was the best-connected woman in the kingdom. And when he graduated from the most exclusive education in the world he was proficient in riding, weapons handling and the wisdom of the Magi. He was tall and handsome and looked just like a king should. He viewed himself as divinely appointed, and almost divinity itself. This man demanded respect.

He had inherited from his father Darius I a sense of global mission and almost immediately after his coronation he'd left for war, where Egypt was quickly and decisively crushed. He then turned his attentions to plans for extending his empire to the west through Greece.

Xerxes certainly enjoyed the high life. From season to season, Persian royalty moved from capital to capital. Life was luxurious, even on the road. Every night, his servants would unload mountains of luggage from the train of camels and mules and pitch a splendid royal tent. Even on the battlefield, the king lived cocooned with his rugs, cushions and perfumed carpets in an apartment made of leather awnings and coloured hangings. Chamber after chamber led away from him, with armed guards at every doorway. He slept on a silver-footed couch covered with beautiful soft linens. Xerxes would only eat food from his own empire so vast amounts of food were transported including his drinking water in great jars filled from a river near Suza. If his lifestyle was like this at war, we don't need too much imagination to envisage life at the palace!

As his entourage travelled, every city in their path was instructed to prepare a royal feast. What a nightmare that must have been. Soldiers, horses, mules and camels needed to be fed and wood provided for fires. The cups on the king's table had to be fashioned out of silver and gold and rugs and carpets of the softest and most luxurious of materials. Then when it was time for the guests to move on they would gather it all up and take it with them.

Invited guests were the princes, officials, military officers and noblemen from all of his 127 provinces. From the furthest corners of his empire they came – Ethiopia to India along the Khorasan Highway and the Royal Road to Suza, the immense winter residence and fortress in the foothills of the Zagros Mountains.

Considering the vast number of guests, and the distances they travelled, it's small wonder this celebration lasted six months.

Party Number 2

> When it was all over, the king gave a special banquet for
> all the palace servants and officials—from the greatest to
> the least. It lasted for seven days and was held at Susa in
> the courtyard of the palace garden. The court-yard was
> decorated with beautifully woven white and blue linen
> hangings, fastened by purple ribbons to silver rings
> embedded in marble pillars. Gold and silver couches
> stood on a mosaic pavement of porphyry, marble, mother-
> of-pearl, and other costly stones. Drinks were served in
> gold goblets of many designs, and there was an abun-
> dance of royal wine, just as the king had commanded.
> (1:5–7)

Perhaps to show his appreciation for all the hard work
put into entertaining, the king rewards his palace staff
with their own banquet – a grand but altogether more
personal event. No one was excluded from servant to
dignitary; no expense spared.

The narrator leads us into the intimate setting of the
courtyard in the palace garden. With awe he draws our
attention to the beautifully woven linen hangings in
white and blue, intricately draped by the careful use of
purple ribbon threaded through silver rings, embedded
in the marble pillars. Next he guides us to the plush gold
and silver couch and points to the vivid mosaic of costly
stones beneath our feet. The party planner's eye to detail
is extended to the table setting. The goblets are not only
solid gold, but also uniquely crafted in design. Quality
wine from the royal cellar flows abundantly, and all are
invited to drink and make their own decision as to when
enough is enough.

For a week even the lowest of servants live like aris-
tocracy. All are encouraged by their host to let their hair

down without any disapproval of their wives, who are entertained separately by the queen.

Queen Vashti refuses

> On the seventh day of the feast, when King Xerxes was half drunk with wine, he told . . . the seven eunuchs who attended him, to bring Queen Vashti to him with the royal crown on her head. He wanted all the men to gaze on her beauty, for she was a very beautiful woman. But when they conveyed the king's order to Queen Vashti, she refused to come. (vv. 10–12a)

This incident still has the power to shock, even centuries later. Like many office parties, the party in the palace ends in regret and shame. With an inflated ego, pumped up with wine and six months of preening, Xerxes oversteps the mark. As energy flags at the end of this seven-day binge, he relies on his wife to spice things up. For the grand finale he has no need for fireworks when he has this beauty to quite literally bring the event to its climax. He envisions the queen herself modelling the royal crown. In the event it's fireworks the guests get, because incredibly, the queen refuses, and the king explodes.

Was she brave, arrogant or stupid? This is the most powerful man in the world. One of his personal inscriptions reads, 'Generously do I repay all those who do well by me.' History tells us that he was delighted with those who loyally served him and would load them down with gifts. Yet, just as quickly, he would viciously turn on those who became too presumptuous.

We don't know if this was the first time she'd held the king's command in contempt and no specific reason is given for Vashti's refusal on this occasion but there are several likely possibilities.

- She was simply exhausted after the strain of entertaining for so long.
- It was 493BC, the same year that her son and the heir to the throne, Artaxerxes, was born. Perhaps she was pregnant or recovering from the birth and she wasn't in tiptop shape physically or emotionally. And so she was incensed at the king's insensitivity.
- She saw the strong link between excessive drinking, unreasonable behavior and sexual immorality. We're told the king was at least half drunk and perhaps if he'd been sober he would never have made this request.
- She was to appear unveiled, which would have been scandalous in the Persian court.
- Many commentators suggest that Vashti was to wear only the crown or that her appearance may have involved a lurid dance or striptease routine. These men were not strangers who she'd never see again but the palace staff. Her dignity was at stake. In future as these subjects bowed, their eyes would gleam with contempt.
- She herself had had too much to drink at her own banquet with the women.

If the results weren't so tragic there is almost something comical about the following scene outlined in Esther 1:13–21.

A king apoplectic with rage shouting petulantly, 'She's spoiled my party!' and his advisers sympathetically and self-importantly stoking up his anger by making Vashti into public enemy number one.

'Why – every family in the empire will be affected by this insubordination. You must stamp it out great King!'

'This could cause the downfall of society.'

Whilst all the time thinking, 'We're having enough trouble with our wives remembering who's boss as it is. What hope will there be after this?'

And so they push for a change in the law that will personally benefit them and every other chauvinist in the empire. It's somewhat surprising that Vashti keeps her head. But the advice the king receives and accepts is still shocking.

Dethronement, banishment and perhaps even separation from her infant son. We can assume she was branded with shame wherever she went. Can you imagine the resentment that came her way from women everywhere now on the receiving end of tightened and restrictive laws?

Some years ago I was leading a women's Bible study in which we discussed Vashti's response to Xerxes' request. One woman felt Vashti should have obeyed. 'Surely, wives are to submit to their husbands in everything,' she insisted. Another held Vashti up as the queen of feminism.

Ephesians 5:21–33 outlines God's plan for marriage. How he created man first to lead, love and protect his wife. How she was designed to be her husband's helper, willingly submitting to his leadership in an intimate relationship that was to be exclusively theirs.

There isn't any evidence to suggest that Vashti had a faith in the true God and it's unlikely she had a biblical understanding of his plan for marriage. It's evident from this account that her culture dictated the rule of man over woman – or at least the rule of king over queen through fear. That culture ordained her main roles were to bring pleasure to the king and to provide him with an heir.

Yet, even among women who belong to God, there are exceptions to the rule of submission. Ephesians 5:22 says

'Wives, submit to your husbands **as to the Lord**.' (NIV, emphasis mine)

In Acts 5:1–11 we read the account of Ananias and Sapphira. In her submission to her husband, Sapphira did not submit as to the Lord. Instead she went along with her husband's lies and was judged by God. Our first responsibility, when there is a conflict between the two, is to submit to God's law, rather than our husbands. That means we are **not** to submit to our husbands if what they demand of us is contrary to how God commands us to behave in his word.

Charles Swindoll in his book on Esther comments:

> What he [Xerxes] asked was not submission; it was sexual slavery. And I applaud Queen Vashti for her courageous decision. Marriage does not give a husband the right or the license to fulfill his basest fantasies by using his wife as a sexual object.[1]

The treatment of Vashti might seem completely alien to us in the twenty-first century, but in much of the world a war is waging against women. In 1993, Secretary General Kofi Annan of the United Nations said 'Violence against women has become the most shameful human rights violation, respecting no distinction of geography, culture or wealth.'[2]

- Women throughout the world suffer more poverty, overwork and discrimination.
- Two thirds of illiterates are women.
- Forced prostitution, sexual assault, rape and wife beating are rampant.
- In Northern India widow burning continues although outlawed and nine thousand brides are killed a year by husbands who want to remarry for a second dowry.

- Young girls in parts of Africa and other Muslim culture countries undergo forced circumcision to curb their sexual desire.
- Hard-core pornography degrades all women, as it instills the view that women's primary value is for sex.
- In Afghanistan many are denied basic medical healthcare and education. Others cannot go out without a male family member, and even then, have to be completely covered from head to foot. Islamic militants threaten women who speak out with death.
- In some cultures, women are not allowed to drive cars.
- Female infanticide, sex selection and abortion are practised around the world, often causing a serious shortage of women. It is estimated that in South and East Asia some one hundred million women are missing due to infanticide, poor maternal health care and nutritional neglect.

Recently I was reminded how this war pervades our so-called civilized society. A scene appeared on a TV drama where a group of male workers stood and chatted as a new female boss walked past. They all leered, apart from one who muttered an insult under his breath. His friend asked, 'So you wouldn't have a go then?' He replied 'Yeah – but I'd tell her she was rubbish afterwards.'

Are twenty-first century's attitudes towards women so different from Persia 483BC? Absolutely not!

What is to be our response as Christian women, we who have been saved by grace, who have God's living and breathing word in our hands, and his spirit in our hearts? Are we to be content with living the way our culture dictates? John Piper writes:

> Over the years I have come to see from Scripture and from life that manhood and womanhood are the beautiful

handiwork of a good and loving God. He designed our differences and they are profound. They are not mere physiological prerequisites for sexual union. They go to the root of our personhood.

He argues that a lack of understanding of those differences in our culture has the consequence of 'more divorce, more homosexuality, more sexual abuse, more promiscuity, more social awkwardness and more emotional distress and suicide that come with with the loss of God-given identity.'[3]

Consider the following questions: Is your view of womanhood influenced by the world around you, tradition or grounded in Scripture? Have you taken time to rediscover and absorb the biblical dignity of woman, appreciating and enjoying both your God given equality and differences with men?

Court protocol around Xerxes was rigorously disciplined. Xerxes focuses on what he sees as the unforgivable sin of broken etiquette but basically he's majoring on minors in order to avoid facing up to his own responsibility and sin. The details are watered down too. He hadn't simply called her before him, but every other Tom, Dick and Harry in the palace.

Perhaps, deep down he realized his request had been unreasonable. Certainly by the beginning of chapter 2 there seems to be some regret but for now he shifts all the blame from himself on to Vashti.

And who among us haven't done that at some point or other? When someone shows us up for what we are or challenges our behaviour it's much easier to shout louder and throw accusations back. I'm reminded of Jesus' words in Matthew 7:3: 'And why worry about a speck in your friend's eye when you have a log in your own?'

His anger dehumanized this woman who moments earlier he'd been so proud to show off. She who'd shared his bed and mothered his son was reduced to a possession of which it was very easy to dispose.

All in all it's an account that leaves a bitter taste in the mouth. Yet despite the sleaze and the scandal there is a ray of hope. Even as Xerxes flexes his chauvinistic muscles there are hints of a greater power at work, found in verse 19 with the suggestion that '. . . you choose another queen more worthy than she.'

The scene is set for the fulfillment of God's perfect plan. Again Swindoll writes:

> Don't fall into the trap of thinking that God is asleep when it comes to nations, or that he is out of touch when it comes to carnal banquets, or that he sits in heaven wringing his hands when it comes to godless rulers (and foolish presidents!) who make unfair, rash or stupid decisions. Mark it down in permanent ink: God is always at work.[4]

A far greater king than Xerxes saw the storm clouds brewing over his people. But he who had promised them hope was even now taking care of that future.

Questions for Personal Reflection

1. How does the Gospel of Christ elevate and liberate women throughout the world? See Gal. 3:28.
2. How will a biblical understanding of the dignity of womanhood affect your life choices and behaviour? (I would recommend further study on this subject. A good starting point is *God's Design for Women* by Sharon James, Evangelical Press)

3. Do you believe that the way we dress often contributes to the dignifying or degrading of women? If so, how and why? Do you believe this is an issue within the church? Is it an issue in the way you personally dress? What guidance are we given in Scripture? See Prov. 7:10; 1 Pet. 3:3–4; 1 Tim. 2:9–10; Prov. 31:22, 25, 30.

4. Perhaps at the moment you're feeling isolated at school, university or at work because you're the only one who's not out binge drinking. Maybe you've already compromised and feel quite comfortable propping up the bar. What does the Bible have to say about drunkenness? See Eph. 5:18–20; Gal. 5:19–21; Is. 5:11; Lk. 21:34; Prov. 23:20, 21, 29, 30. How many of these dangers are demonstrated in Esther 1? Honestly think through the implications for your own life. Are there changes you need to be making in this area?

5. How does this passage give you hope?

Holding on to Dignity

☞ *Read ESTHER 2*

There hadn't been a queen for four years. Pumped up with a war to fight against the Greeks, Xerxes had had enough to keep him busy. Against all the odds, he'd been defeated and, to add insult to injury, had to rush back to Babylon to deal with an attempted coup. Not surprisingly, it's a different character we encounter at the beginning of chapter 2: 'But after Xerxes' anger had cooled, he began thinking about Vashti and what she had done and the decree he had made.' (Esth. 2:1)

His image has taken such a hammering and is perhaps further dented by the absence of a queen. Do you detect a note of melancholy, an air of vulnerability and loneliness, and a hint of despair? This man is hurting, but there's no one to give him the comfort for which he longs. The great king is human after all, and as he reflects on his mistakes (it's only taken four years to get there) he realizes he can't get Vashti back. He's at a loss.

This time, advice comes from his close personal attendants, rather than his top advisers.

> So his attendants suggested, "Let us search the empire to find beautiful young virgins for the king. Let the king

appoint agents in each province to bring these beautiful young women into the royal harem at Susa. Hegai, the eunuch in charge, will see that they are all given beauty treatments. After that, the young woman who pleases you most will be made queen instead of Vashti." This advice was very appealing to the king, so he put the plan into effect immediately. (2:2–4)

Why was this advice so appealing to the king? Obviously the prospect of endless nights of passion with the most pampered and sexually prepared young virgins of the kingdom was exciting for this red-blooded king. But then again, didn't he already have a harem of beauties that waited for his call? In his pain, it was stability and companionship he longed for, not only sex. He wanted a wife again.

We may not approve of his way of getting one (selfishly trying each woman out like test-driving cars and discarding the worst performers), but we can recognize his need as one natural for a man designed that way by his Creator.

And the LORD God said, "It is not good for the man to be alone. I will make a companion who will help him." So the LORD God formed from the soil every kind of animal and bird. He brought them to Adam to see what he would call them, and Adam chose a name for each one. He gave names to all the livestock, birds, and wild animals. But still there was no companion suitable for him. So the LORD God caused Adam to fall into a deep sleep. He took one of Adam's ribs and closed up the place from which he had taken it. Then the LORD God made a woman from the rib and brought her to Adam.

"At last!" Adam exclaimed. "She is part of my own flesh and bone! She will be called 'woman,' because she was taken out of man." This explains why a man leaves his father and mother and is joined to his wife, and the two are united into one. Now, although Adam and his wife were both naked, neither of them felt any shame. (Gen. 2:18–25)

Our world tells us that sex satisfies. Xerxes proves it doesn't.

The Genesis account shows categorically that God is pro-sex. He himself designed intimacy between a man and a woman. Tony Payne and Phillip Jensen write in their book *Pure Sex*:

> In the garden, God creates sex as a profound interpersonal act between the man and the woman. It is not a casual or neutral bodily function, like shaking hands or going to the toilet. It is an act of the deepest personal intimacy and self-giving. If it is working properly, sex bonds us to the other person. We become not only physically one with them, but deeply emotionally one with them as well. And once a sexual relationship has begun, it cannot be ended without grief.[1]

That's why for Xerxes, sexual relationships outside of his marriage have left him cold. Why he longs for a wife.

The wheels are set in motion.

Introducing Mordecai

When we reach verse 5 it's as if a cool and refreshing breeze blows across the scene. Up to this point, the red-hot intrigue of the Persian court has dominated the book. God hasn't been mentioned. In fact, considering the state of exiled Israel, many would have been tempted to believe that Israel's God was dead. But although he isn't mentioned by name, we are pointed to him. We're introduced to Mordecai, and we are reminded that despite everything God is very much alive, and so are his people.

What do we learn about this man?

As a Jew he's the genuine article
His family name is Kish, which can be traced all the way back to King Saul's father in 1100BC. He was the fourth generation of deported Jews, his great-grandfather actually experiencing the exile to Babylon. After Cyrus of Persia conquered the Babylonians in 539BC, the Jews were scattered through the new empire, and that's why we find Mordecai's family living in Susa, right under the king's nose.

He's living proof that God keeps his promises
Do you remember that promise made to the exiles? 'I know the plans I have for you,' says the Lord. 'They are plans for good and not for disaster, to give you a future and a hope.' Mordecai's very existence proves God's faithfulness and as we will discover Mordecai's family are not the only Jews who have survived.

He's a family man with a big heart
'This man had a beautiful and lovely young cousin, Hadassah, who was also called Esther. When her father and mother had died, Mordecai adopted her into his family and raised her as his own daughter.' (2:7)

When his aunt and uncle died he took their child in. Not as 'Cinderella-style' servant but as an adopted and highly valued daughter.

The famous saying goes, 'Behind every good man is a good woman.' There's a lot of truth in that. I recently read a biography on Clementine Churchill (wife of Winston). I was mesmerized by her support, love and wisdom. But when did you last see a statue of her or a TV documentary on her? Most of the acclaim went to her husband but I'm convinced that Winston wouldn't have achieved half of what he did without her, and that God in his providence, placed them both in our world as a means of our deliverance from the Nazis.

In this case there is some role reversal. I think we can safely say that behind this woman, Esther, there's a good man. Mordecai's that man, and although the book's named after Esther, he's introduced to us, as a most noteworthy and valuable character. We'll explore more of Mordecai's influence later.

Introducing Esther

> 'This man had a beautiful and lovely young cousin, Hadassah, who was also called Esther.' (Esth. 2:7a)

Her beauty is heavily emphasized in this verse. Who would use 'beautiful' and 'lovely' in the same sentence? The NIV has 'lovely in form and features'. The original text is 'beautiful in form and lovely to look at.' Even her name conveys beauty. Her Jewish name, Hadassah, comes from the word for the myrtle bush and means 'fragrance'. Esther, her Persian name, means 'star' which could also refer to the star-like shapes of the myrtle flowers.

Everything about her is gorgeous. Even the narrator is entranced with her, and this even before the palace beauticians have got their eager hands on her.

Our culture is obsessed with beauty. In a recent *OK!* magazine the articles are entitled:

FROM UGLY DUCKLINGS TO BEAUTIFUL SWANS – LOOK AT ME NOW!

Some stars weren't born stunning – they needed a bit of help here and there to blossom . . .

CELEB MUMS! How they lost the baby bulge.

THE GOLDEN GLOBES. OK! looks at the winners and losers in the style stakes.[2]

The Persian court was no different. The Persians were also obsessed with physical appearance. Every nobleman kept a make-up artist in his train. The must-have fashion item was a pair of platform heels and false beards and moustaches were so valued that the exchequer classed them as a taxable item.[3]

'As a result of the king's decree, Esther, along with many other young women, was brought to the king's harem at the fortress of Susa and placed in Hegai's care.' (v. 8) There can be no doubt of Esther's beauty for her to be so noticed and taken to the fortress.

At first glance, Esther's story is appealing and exciting, a true 'rags to riches' story – the stuff that *OK!* magazine would lap up. Can you imagine the shots the paparazzi would take, as the women paraded up the red carpeted steps into the palace, the discussions and articles about the hairstyles, make-up techniques and diets of these new celebs?

'Tell us your story!' The reporters would shout from the sidelines.

'How can we be like you?'

Imagine some of the answers.

'I was just in the right place at the right time,' one might coo.

'Daddy works at the Palace,' admits another.

'It's fate! I always knew I was born for this.'

'You just need to go with your dream.'

'You have to believe in yourself!'

But take time to look into the eyes of one young woman, and perhaps they'd remind us that this isn't necessarily the fairytale lifestyle it appears (vv. 12–14).

Esther has been taken from those she loves, probably against her will, with no chance of return. Surrounded by women from many different cultures and religions she's introduced to pagan surroundings from which there can be no escape. Rather than the companionship of a Jewish marriage and the joy of family life in a normal home, she looks forward to the likely life of a harem – dutiful sex without love and valuable only as long as her beauty lasts. Can you imagine the cattiness and jealousy that would exist in such an environment?

Added to all this is the suggestion of danger, if the truth of her nationality becomes public. 'Esther had not told anyone of her nationality and family background, for Mordecai had told her not to.' (v. 10)

What a terrifying ordeal this must have been for this young Jewess.

At my local gym there are four TV screens, BBC1, ITV, Sky Sports, and a music channel, MTV. If I sneak a look at any of the men using the gym, I can almost guarantee which screen their eyes are on. No! They are not making the most of free Sky sport. Most are completely focused on the beautiful gyrating bodies of the female singers on MTV. Any child watching, whatever their age, would have their own short course in the skills of seduction. Last week as I pounded angrily on my treadmill, I prayed, 'Lord, how can my kids be kept pure in this society? How can Christian young women and men remain true to you despite our culture?'

Esther gives me hope. Despite her surroundings and all she had to endure and even engage in, she comes out the other side with dignity and strength. Far from being conformed to the Persian worldview, she does great things for God. How could this be?

1. Dignity comes from knowledge of the loving Creator

She was chosen and created by God. Knowing we're created lovingly is to know dignity.

Esther was a Jewess – all God's promises to the nation applied to her as an individual. Her ancestor King David, who frequently claimed God's promises as his own in the Psalms, remembered that a man and woman's true worth is grounded in the plans of the Creator.

> You made all the delicate, inner parts of my body
> and knit me together in my mother's womb.
> Thank you for making me so wonderfully complex!
> Your workmanship is marvelous—and how well I
> know it.
> You watched me as I was being formed in utter seclusion,
> as I was woven together in the dark of the womb.
> You saw me before I was born.
> Every day of my life was recorded in your book.
> Every moment was laid out
> before a single day had passed. (Psalm 139)

Be honest! How often do you think about your appearance? Are you content with how you look? If you keep fit, what drives you? Is it the desire to glorify your Creator by looking after the body he's loaned you, or to glorify yourself by striving for that perfect physique?

When you're feeling sad is your immediate response to go shopping or get some beauty treatments to cheer yourself up? Can you go shopping without making a purchase and return home without feelings of dissatisfaction?

A recent survey showed the average British woman worries about the size and shape of her body every 15 minutes.[4] David's words make this obsession seem pathetic to say the least. He looks beyond the trivialities of outward beauty alone and recognizes:

- **His Creator's care.** He wasn't thrown together in a hurry or haphazardly mixed together. He praises God that he was lovingly 'knitted' together, and 'woven'. God was following an intricate pattern, in his chosen colours and shape. David recognizes that he is the Creator's masterpiece.

  I read of a woman who became so disenchanted with her body after gaining some weight that she avoided her husband's advances for intimacy. His tough but wise advice to her was to stand naked before a full length mirror with verse 14 of this Psalm taped to it. From the top of her head right down to her toes she thanked God for all his careful attention to every detail of her body and the purposes for which each part had been designed. After a while she prayed: 'God, forgive me. I've been focusing on all the wrong things. I've obsessed about trivia, when my body has been personally fashioned by You. I give thanks to You. Wonderful are Your works, for I am fearfully and wonderfully made.'[5]
- **His Creator's care for his future.** 'Every day of my life was recorded in your book.' God didn't write David's story, in retrospect like a biography, but he wrote it before he'd even lived a day of it. How amazing is that?

God's words for David's book were carefully contemplated, his thoughts coherent. The book made
sense. It had a beginning and an end and the plot in
between never went off on a tangent. The Creator
carefully fits the person with the plan. He does not
make mistakes.

Most of us probably wish at times we were more beautiful, but God created Esther's beauty for a purpose. Not
to fulfil her own ambitions but to be used for his glory.

God looked out for her all the way through, causing
even Hegai, the eunuch in charge, to view her with
favourable eyes and to take special care of her.

2. Dignity is promoted by wise, consistent and loving advice

Esther was blessed with a great mentor. Mordecai had
loved and grounded her well. We can be confident of his
fundamental teaching before Esther goes to the palace,
because of his actions and wise words throughout the
book. His most famous words when tragedy strikes are
'Who can say but that you have been elevated to the
palace for just such a time as this?' (Esth. 4:14)

I don't believe this man would have willingly sent her
into this environment, but he trusted in God's sovereignty
in the matter.

When Caitlin, my daughter, went on her first summer
camp at the age of ten, I prepared her the best I could, as
I overloaded her case, and then overloaded her head,
with instructions and advice. Then I fretted and stewed,
watching the clock the entire time she was gone, trying
to work out what she'd be doing at each precise moment.

The Persian court was no summer camp run by
Christians. There was no Bible teaching here. Rather, it

was a place of political intrigue. Mordecai's precious Esther was being cared for by the godless and educated in the art of seduction.

She was being prepared for a man who was not committed to God's plan for marriage and worse – one who was not a follower of the true God.

Again and again, God had commanded his people throughout the Old Testament not to marry partners from other nations. Again and again he'd warned them that they'd be led astray by their pagan practices.

In fact, their disobedience of this very command was one of the fundamental reasons the Jews had ended up in exile (In Josh. 23:6–16 Joshua warns them that they would lose their land). Mordecai was reasonably concerned for her welfare: 'Every day Mordecai would take a walk near the courtyard of the harem to ask about Esther and to find out what was happening to her.' (2:11)

Although Esther was no longer in his care, Mordecai didn't abandon her. He was an exemplary father.

- He took time out for her
- Kept himself informed
- Showed his concern
- Was consistently and regularly there for her
- Continued to advise her (2:10)
- Continued to protect her from danger when he could (2:10)

In Esther chapter 1 we saw how a woman, even a queen, was considered little more than a disposable item. Yet in chapter 2 Mordecai reminded Esther of her true value in every way he could.

Here was one qualified by his presence to give good advice. If we skip down to verse 19 we find that Mordecai later secured a job as a palace official to be near her. When we get to verse 21, we discover that his advice was well worth listening to. Re-read verses 21 to 23.

- Here was a man of principle. He practiced what he preached. Not only did this loyal subject save the king from assassination, he protected Esther's position and enhanced her reputation by passing the message on through her.
- Mordecai didn't have tunnel vision. He wasn't so taken up with his family concerns that he was blinded to everything else going on in the world. He viewed life through a wide-angle lens that made his advice balanced and wise on a minute-by-minute basis.

How can we take on Mordecai's role in the lives of our own daughters? I'm not only talking about biological daughters here (although the challenge certainly applies). Of course Mordecai wasn't Esther's mother but in her absence he did his best to fill the void. Is there anyone in who you are investing time and energy? Not for what you'll get out of the relationship but because you have a deep concern for that person's well-being and growth? Whatever age we are or however long we have been Christians, if we look around at church or in our Christian Union there is nearly always someone who is younger than us and could benefit from practical concern and love.

3. Dignity is enhanced by a humble response

This young woman is distinctive and Hegai spots the difference straight away.

Hegai was very impressed with Esther and treated her kindly. He quickly ordered a special menu for her and provided her with beauty treatments. He also assigned her seven maids specially chosen from the king's palace, and he moved her and her maids into the best place in the harem. (2:9)

There were many new beauties in the palace, but Hegai was on the lookout for a wife and a queen. A bimbo wouldn't do. He was looking beyond the superficial attributes and beneath the cosmetics he saw her promise. Verse 9 describes her at the beginning of the year, before a year of pampering and attention. Verses 15 to 20 describe her situation by the end of the year.

Esther's advancement is spectacular. She's been plucked from obscurity and propelled towards glittering royalty and public acclaim. The king was captivated with her and so was everyone else.

Whilst sitting on a cliff overlooking a Welsh beach I overheard a family discussing the latest gossip concerning local Swansea girl/Hollywood star Catherine Zeta Jones. It concluded with the grandmother's decisive words, 'That girl's got too big for her boots!'

I wouldn't like to say whether that's true or not, but that accusation could never be levelled at Esther.

Let's look at her characteristics and response.

1. She was courageous
Despite what could be described as a terrifying ordeal, Esther remains poised and quietly confident. How do we know? She would never have been selected by Hegai for advancement, or the king for his queen had she been cowered with fear.

2. She was flexible
She found herself in a situation she probably didn't choose and one she couldn't change. But she humbly and graciously accepted her lot and coped with it.

3. She was discreet, in speech and appearance

She knew how to keep her mouth shut. She kept her nationality secret for over a year and later in the story she knows how to handle herself in a crisis.

When it comes to her big night with the king, we don't find her obsessively preparing herself, shopping in the royal mall for couture clothing and rare eye-catching jewellery. She wasn't one to flaunt herself. She quietly trusted the advice of her friend and put her trust in her Creator to handle the future. I can't be sure, but when she entered the king's suite, I bet she was nothing but herself, and it was that transparency and purity as well as her outward beauty that captivated him.

4. She was wise

She recognized that even the queen needs good advice. As she surfed high on a wave of success, Esther could easily have severed her links with Mordecai. She could have treated him as an embarrassment, her background one that could only hinder her career. She could have thrown herself wholeheartedly into the fashionable lifestyle and worshipped beauty and materialism. Esther did none of these things. Even though she was free of his power she willingly placed herself under the advice she treasured.

Consider the following questions.

'How do I keep my faith in this culture? How do I keep my head in the dizzy heights of success? How do I discern whether to walk through a door of opportunity? How do I remain focused on the road ahead when voices call out from every side? How do I continue to walk with dignity and trust when the future looks bleak and loneliness and despair close in?'

Now read some advice given by King Solomon in the book of Proverbs 13.

'Pride leads to arguments; those who take advice are wise.' (13:10).

'The advice of the wise is like a life-giving fountain; those who accept it avoid the snares of death.' (13:14)

'If you ignore criticism, you will end in poverty and disgrace; if you accept criticism, you will be honoured.' (13:18).

'Whoever walks with the wise will become wise; whoever walks with fools will suffer harm.' (13:20).

This king recognized the value of good friends. Queen Esther identified her vulnerability and was aware of hidden dangers all around her. Do we?

These verses state categorically that we all need good, wise and godly friends. Without them we are in grave danger. Those of us who've just left home for the first time and are enjoying our new freedom and privacy, are especially vulnerable. With parents and respected church leaders and friends far away we need to make accountability a priority. At university, finding a truth-teaching church, where the fellowship is warm, and, if possible, joining the Christian Union can't be safely put off for long. We need to recognize our weakness, we need to pray that God will provide us with a wise counsellor.

Often, the older we get the less we see the need for accountability. But if that's so, we may be older, but we're certainly not wiser.

Even missionaries, Christian workers and minister's wives need it, however high the pedestal others put us on. We're bound to fall off without wise friends who will keep our feet firmly rooted on the ground while challenging us to grow and not to become self-satisfied.

So ask yourself . . .

- Who is there that asks you the hard questions about the parts of your life you like to keep private?

- Who loves you in a way that has proven they want the very best for you?
- Who do you know with a wide and balanced perspective?
- Who do you respect in terms of their own consistent Christian walk?
- Who do you know who will always tell you the truth, even when it's hard to give and even harder to accept?
- Who do you know who sees your God-given potential, even when you can't, and will encourage you to reach it?
- Who helps you to love Christ more?

This is the woman and these are the women you need to be accountable to. If no one springs to mind, pray for the provision of such a friend and seek to be such a friend to others.

Notice I used the word 'women'. Apart from husbands and family members, we need to restrict this kind of spiritually intimate relationship to other women to safeguard ourselves sexually and emotionally. There is pure wisdom in Paul's words in Titus when he writes:

> Similarly, teach the older women to live in a way that is appropriate for someone serving the Lord. They must not go around speaking evil of others and must not be heavy drinkers. Instead, they should teach others what is good. These older women must train the younger women to love their husbands and their children, to live wisely and be pure, to take care of their homes, to do good, and to be submissive to their husbands. Then they will not bring shame on the word of God. (Tit. 2:3–5)

5. *She refused to be degraded*
The seedy part of this story tends to be glossed over in our evangelical churches. Up until recently, I actually

thought that this queen was selected on her looks alone. As the shocking reality sunk in that this was a *sex* as well as a beauty contest, I've struggled to understand how any woman like Esther could keep her dignity in such circumstances. Is it too extreme to call this a form of sexual abuse? I think not.

I doubt she had much choice in the matter and although God graciously allowed and preordained her to be chosen as queen and wife to this man, she wasn't married to him, and didn't even know him, when she had sex with him that first time.

A friend of mine Susie shares the devastating effects sexual abuse has had on her:

> Up to the age of twelve, I underwent sexual abuse but never thought to seek help. Throughout my teenage years and early adulthood I suffered with no self-worth, a great lack of confidence, obsessive attitudes and actions, whilst feeling completely unloved and unlovable. I only began to seek help when I became so depressed that it began to seriously affect my work.

Corrie Ten Boon, a prisoner in Ravensbruck concentration camp with her sister Betsie, describes the following ordeal in her autobiography, *The Hiding Place*.[6]

> Fridays – the recurrent humiliation of medical inspection. The hospital corridor in which we waited was unheated, and a tall chill had settled into the walls. Still we were forbidden even to wrap ourselves in our own arms, but had to maintain our erect, hands-at-sides position as we filed slowly past a phalanx of grinning guards. How there could have been any pleasure in the sight of these stick-thin legs and hunger-bloated stomachs I could not imagine. Surely there is no more wretched sight than the

human body unloved and uncared for. Nor could I see the necessity for the complete undressing: when we finally reached the examining room a doctor looked down each throat, another – a dentist presumably – at our teeth, a third in between each finger. And that was all. We trooped again down the long, cold corridor and picked up our X-marked dresses at the door.

We don't know the details of Esther's night. We don't know how she dealt with her fear in the year leading up to it. Nor how she coped with her feelings afterwards although I would imagine that at times she felt shame, guilt and burning anger.

This is not God's plan for sex and although he doesn't deliver her physically from the experience we need to be reminded that as a holy God, he is angry at all sin including all forms of abusive behaviour. Even kings like Xerxes will account for their actions before him. We do in our society today have some means of legal protection and recourse and where possible these means should be used.

But how does that help with the shame of it all?

1 John 1:9 promises us that, 'If we confess our sins to him, he is faithful and just to forgive us and to cleanse us from every wrong.' Forgiveness is not just a New Testament concept. God promises Jeremiah, 'I will forgive their wickedness and will never again remember their sins.' (Jer. 31:34)

Micah asks:

'Where is another God like you, who pardons the sins of the survivors among his people? You cannot stay angry with your people forever, because you delight in showing mercy. Once again you will have compassion on us. You will trample our sins under your feet and throw them into the depths of the ocean!' (Mich. 7:18–20)

If God willingly forgives us for our sins, doesn't he even more willingly cleanse us from the shame we feel as a result of other's sin against us?

The guilt of sexual sin, especially it seems for us women (whether our own or that practised against us), either hardens us or crushes us, often ruining the delight of married sex.

Esther was neither hardened nor crushed, as we will see through the book. I don't know the process she went through to get there but I believe she knew God's cleansing power and love in a way that actually strengthened her dignity. Below are three different accounts in their own words of how God enabled three different women to come to terms with their past. The processes are different. The result is the same.

Corrie Ten Boon's story

> . . . it was one of these mornings while we were waiting, shivering, in the corridor, that yet another page in the Bible leapt into life for me.
>
> He hung naked on the cross.
>
> I had not known – I had not thought . . . The paintings, the carved crucifixes showed at the least a scrap of cloth. But this, I suddenly knew, was the respect and reverence of the artist. But oh – at the time itself, on that other Friday morning – there had been no reverence. No more than I saw in the faces around us now.
>
> I leaned toward Betsie, ahead of me in line. Her shoulder blades stood out sharp and thin beneath her blue-mottled skin.
>
> "Betsie, they took *His* clothes too."

> Ahead of me I heard a little gasp. "Oh, Corrie. And I never thanked Him . . ."

After the war she travelled to Germany to speak. At the end of a service one of the S.S. guards who had mocked them approached her. As she was transported back to the memories of humiliation:

> He came up to me as the church was emptying, beaming and bowing. "How grateful I am for your message *Fraulein*," he said. "To think that, as you say, He has washed my sins away!"
>
> His hand was thrust out to shake mine...Even as the angry, vengeful thoughts boiled through me, I saw the sin of them. Jesus Christ had died for this man; was I going to ask for more? Lord Jesus, I prayed, forgive me and help me to forgive him.
>
> I tried to smile, I struggled to raise my hand. I could not. I felt nothing, not the slightest spark of warmth or charity. And so again I breathed a silent prayer. Jesus, I cannot forgive him. Give me Your forgiveness.
>
> As I took his hand the most incredible thing happened. From my shoulder along my arm and through my hand a current seemed to pass from me to him, while into my heart sprang a love for this stranger that almost overwhelmed me.
>
> And so I discovered that it is not on our forgiveness any more than on our goodness that the world's healing hinges, but on His. When He tells us to love our enemies, He gives, along with that command, the love itself.

The whole concept of forgiveness can be much more complex when the perpetrator is unrepentant, but don't you agree that Corrie's experience is the most remarkable display of God-given dignity as he enabled her to forgive?

Susie's story

Eventually, with the help of Christian counselling, friendship and medication I began to face the past, dealing with its hurt and complexities, but primarily I saw how it was controlling my present actions. I began to see my situation and myself as God saw me.

For the first time I realized that he loved me for who I was, and that I didn't have to earn His affection by endless activities and good works. In fact, he had loved me from before I was born, so I hadn't been able to do anything to cause him to feel that way about me.

Relationships had always been a problem to me. At times I feared to let people in. Then, at other times, I felt very possessive towards them, to the point of obsession, fearing they would leave or hate me, so I constantly had to do things to prevent this. This began to change when I saw in the Bible that the Lord sticks closer than family or friends and that he will NEVER LEAVE me, regardless of how I viewed myself, or what I did or didn't do.

Previously, I had sought confirmation of my worth in the way others responded to the things I did, but I began to see that I could never be good enough, often enough, to receive the affirmation I required. But then I realized that to God I was *always* precious. This took a tremendous amount of pressure off me, as I no longer had to 'perform' constantly. At any time, under any circumstances, God valued me.

I used to feel the need to control everyone and everything around me, as it was the only way I could guarantee giving my life the security I required. This is no longer the case as I have complete confidence that God is in control, not only of my life but also of the entire universe, and that he will work all things together for good for those who love him, as well as his own glory. God has my interests at heart and he knows no unkindness. I can't control everything all the time so there is no point in trying. But God can!

My past hasn't changed – it never will. But with God's help I no longer have to live in the shadow it casts, and my future is secure. It's in his hands.

Helen Rosevere's story

In the 1960s, Dr Helen Rosevere served as a missionary in the Congo. During that time she went through many traumatic experiences including kidnap and rape. In an interview for the 2006 London Women's Convention, Jonathan Carswell asked her how she'd come to terms with it all.

She explained that *before* she went on the mission field, as Jesus had prayed in the garden before his crucifixion 'Not my will but yours be done,' she'd told God that she had wanted that to be true of her. That helped her to accept her trials as his will, even though she didn't really understand how it could be.

During her suffering God kept reminding her of the verse 'My grace is sufficient' 'even when something was really difficult and there was a beat up or something really harsh there was certainly "My grace is sufficient" and it was . . .'

And afterwards:

> Later looking back . . . he said, "Can you thank me?" Initially of course I said, "No way" but then I looked at it and thought "I'm not thanking him for the evil. You only thank God for the good things he gives." He said, "But can you thank me for trusting you?"
>
> That was a revolutionary thought to me. I'd always thought of me trusting him but not him trusting me. He

said, "Can you thank me for trusting you with this experience even if I never tell you why?"

And that brought it's own peace. As soon as one said, "Thank you, I don't know what you're doing Lord and why you're allowing this, but if it's part of your purposes, thank you for trusting me." Immediately he poured in his peace and there was an acceptance that wasn't difficult.[7]

Questions for Personal Reflection

1. Read Genesis 2:18–25 again. How do we know that God is compassionate and desired the best for his people during this creation account? Why was woman created and what was Adam's response to her? How do we know that God intended this to be a monogamous relationship?
2. Pray through Psalm 139:13–16. How do these truths change the perspective on your life? Be specific about your past and present struggles.
3. How can you develop relationships and implement a strategy that responds to the need of mentoring and accountability?

Standing up to Monsters

☞ *Read ESTHER 3*

Haman had hit the big time. This son of Hammedtha basked in the glory bestowed upon him by none other than King Xerxes. He'd been promoted to Prime Minister, but was treated as royalty. Xerxes himself commanded his officials to bow before him. All obeyed, except one man. Mordecai stood erect not only the first time Haman strutted past, but on every occasion afterwards, despite the persuasion and jibes of his colleagues.

'What's your problem Mordecai?'

'Are you mad?'

'I thought Jews were supposed to be model citizens.'

'Just a small bow won't harm.'

Mordecai had worked hard to protect Esther, so why was he now so openly courting danger right under the king's nose? There was no possibility that his behaviour would go unnoticed. Surely he should compromise his beliefs for the sake of his young cousin. Did he view himself as too great, as Esther's relation to bow to the Prime Minister?

That can't be right! We know that he'd never used Esther's position for self-promotion. Their relationship had been kept strictly under wraps. Neither was he standing in rebellion against the king and his authority – we saw how in the last chapter he'd intervened to save the king's life. His loyalty was beyond question.

To find the reason behind Mordecai's behaviour, we need to look at Haman the way the wise Mordecai saw him.

Haman Exposed

1. Haman was an Agagite (and Mordecai was a Benjamanite)

A tribal feud had raged between the Agagites and Benjamanites for generations. In 1 Samuel 15, we read of an encounter between another Benjamanite, King Saul, and King Agag of the Amalekites.

Samuel said to Saul:

> This is what the LORD Almighty says: 'I have decided to punish the nation of Amalek for opposing Israel when they came from Egypt. Now go and completely destroy the entire Amalekite nation—men, women, children, babies, cattle, sheep, camels, and donkeys. (1 Sam. 15:2–3)

We need to be clear here that this nation must have been pure evil for God to have instructed Saul so clearly and severely. In verse 7 he makes a good start in executing God's justice. By verse 9 however, his religious zeal is failing: 'Saul and his men spared Agag's life and kept the best of the sheep and cattle, the fat calves and lambs – everything, in fact, that appealed to them. They destroyed only what was worthless or of poor quality.'

God was angry, sending Samuel to convey his displeasure and rejection of Saul's kingship. Then comes the crunch for King Agag.

> Samuel said "Bring King Agag to me." Agag arrived full of smiles, for he thought, "Surely the worst is over and I have been spared!" But Samuel said, "As your sword has killed the sons of many mothers now your mother will be childless." And Samuel cut Agag to pieces before the LORD at Gilgal. (15:32, 33)

But this wasn't historical hostility alone.

2. Haman was a Jew-hater

He didn't keep his anti-semitism a secret. In Esther 3:4 we read that the officials, 'spoke to Haman about this to see if he would tolerate Mordecai's conduct, since Mordecai had told them he was a Jew.'

They knew that the secret of Mordecai's nationality was dynamite as far as Haman was concerned. By snitching to the Prime Minister they fuelled his hatred and showed themselves willing to join him in his anti-semitic club, even if they weren't already sympathisers. Haman doesn't seem to have noticed Mordecai standing tall behind the grovelling masses, until it's pointed out to him.

The result? Haman completely and utterly overreacts. He completely loses it. Not only is he apoplectic with rage towards Mordecai, the Benjamanite, but with the entire Jewish race.

Antagonism had thrived between the nations since soon after Moses had led the Israelites out of Egypt. We read in Exodus 17:8–16 that the Amalekites had launched an unprovoked and vicious attack upon them.

Deuteronomy 25:18 tells us the reason for this: 'They had no fear of God.'

God was so angry with this that he commanded, '. . . you are to destroy the Amalekites and erase their memory from under heaven. Never forget this!' (Deut. 25:19b)

Haman stands by his predecessors showing that he has no fear of God either as the depths of his hostility towards the Jews is revealed. Scripture labels him as 'the enemy of the Jews' for the first time in Esther 3:10, and then another four times afterwards.

We should be able to understand Mordecai's refusal to bow to this man, but we can still marvel at the courage it takes.

Paul Schneider was a young church minister in Germany. From early on in Hitler's rule Paul spoke out against Nazi policies, refusing to use the greeting, 'Heil Hitler.'

He was arrested and imprisoned twice for his stand, released the second time only on the condition that he accept an expulsion order from the Rhineland.

His wife Gretel hoped he would give in and move away. But Paul had already decided not to give in to the Gestapo bullying. In despair she asked, 'Paul, don't you think abut the children and me? Paul, don't you love us?'

He held her to his chest and sobbed, 'My darling, I have never loved you or the children more than on that night of decision. I wept for you.'

For almost two years Paul was held in Buchenwald Concentration camp. Despite repeated taunting, torture and extreme beating he refused to sign the documents that would free him, preaching even at the bars of his cell. He said, 'Someone has to preach in this hell.'

Finally the camp doctor lethally injected him with a massive dose of strophanthin, leaving Gretel to bring up their six young children alone.

A survivor of the camp commented, 'In my estimation he was the only man in Germany who, overcoming all human fear, so consistently took on himself the cross of Christ even to death.'[1]

Mordecai had watched the assent of Haman and studied his character. His courage, shown by his refusal to bow, caused a reaction in Haman which revealed his true character.

3. Haman's character

- **He was a bitter and vengeful man.** His grudges drove a very personal agenda. Here he was at the beginning of his ministerial term of office. He held the opportunity and duty to serve and enhance both king and country. Instead, we find him plotting a scheme that will only benefit himself and damage society at large.
- **Haman had a terrible temper.** He erupted immediately. All the bitterness and hatred that had writhed for years exploded, causing devastation all around him. His reaction remind me of the verse: 'As the beating of cream yields butter, and a blow to the nose causes bleeding, so anger causes quarrels.' (Prov. 30:33)
- **Haman was a fool.** His foolishness also told him he was in control, and that he was in effect God. Psalm 14:1 says 'Only fools say in their hearts, "There is no God".' (NLT).
- Despite wealth and power, he was dissatisfied with what he had.
- **Haman was devious.** He twisted the truth and cashed in on the time when the king was likely to have felt vulnerable – after a failed campaign in Greece that was immediately followed by an attempted coup in Babylon and a failed assassination attempt by two of his own eunuchs.

'There is a certain race of people scattered through all the provinces of your empire. Their laws are different from those of any other nation, and they refuse to obey the laws of the king. So it is not in the king's interest to let them live.' (Esth. 3:8)

Contrary to these words, all the evidence around this time in the books of Ezra and Nehemiah indicate that the Jews were a submissive and honourable nation. In the multicultural society of Persia there must have been *many* different nationalities that practised their individual customs.

Haman feigned complete devotion to the king even offering to foot the bill himself for this major operation. I think he was bluffing. He knew the king wouldn't accept his cash but it did the trick. Then he turned his attention to the citizens of Persia.

He carefully worked up their patriotism, by marginalizing the Jews. He then appealed to their greed, commanding them to claim their intended victims' wealth for themselves.

Diet Eman aided the Dutch Resistance helping to save hundreds of Jews during the Nazi occupation of her country. She writes:

> Right from the beginning, the Occupation created ambiguities, arguments, and difficult struggles within Christian circles . . . Part of the struggle, the moral struggle, was the belief that what had happened in our little country was in fact ordained by God; some people claimed that we shouldn't interfere with what went on because the occupation itself was God's will.[2]

If Christians have battled with these issues then Haman can't have found it too difficult to convince the godless citizens of Persia.

- **He was relentless and knew no mercy.** In verse 13, we see the instructions were translated into every language and went to every area. The command went from the very top (the king himself) to every official and worked its way down to the ordinary people. There was to be no mercy. This was a pure revenge attack. All Jews were targeted – young, old, men, women, and children were to be executed and all in a single day.
- **Haman had no conscience.** After the couriers rode out of a reeling and bewildered Suza with their grim news, Haman sat down with his best buddy Xerxes to drink. He celebrated while a nation shook. He congratulated himself instead of reassuring the people he was called to serve.

Goering the second-in-command to Hitler once said, 'I have no conscience. My conscience is Hitler.' So here sat two powerful men, getting drunk without a tender conscience between them.

Throughout this time Mordecai stood firm. He recognized the need to stand firm for his God, whatever the consequences for himself, Esther and ultimately his people. Although he had no idea quite how violently Haman would react, he knew the risks.

It's important that we understand that behind the scenes a far greater battle was raging. This was a war between Satan and the God of Israel. Satan wanted to obliterate the Jews so there could be no Messiah to bring salvation to this lost world. He never wanted our salvation. This battle was for our souls as well as the lives of the Jews.

Sometimes as Christians we seem shocked when the world doesn't automatically appreciate us for being good citizens. We're bemused when we're blamed for society's problems and accused of being narrow-minded. We panic that society around us is becoming more secular and anti-God. Yet this is how it has always been since Cain persecuted his brother Abel because his own works were evil, while Abel's were righteous (Gen. 4:2–7).

John writes:

> See how very much our heavenly Father loves us, for he allows us to be called his children, and we really are! But the people who belong to this world don't know God, so they don't understand that we are his children. (1 Jn. 3:1)

So what encourages us to stand when we are being persecuted or marginalized? The love of a father has been lavished upon us. The wonderful and amazing truth that we are the children of God helps us to see beyond our present struggle, to the glory that will be ours in eternity. The children of God *can't* be destroyed.

Jesus wisely tells us in Matthew that:

> God blesses those who are persecuted
> because they live for God . . .
>
>   God blesses you when you are mocked and persecuted and lied about because you are my followers. Be happy about it! Be very glad! For a great reward awaits you in heaven. And remember, the ancient prophets were persecuted, too. (5:10–12)

When my children were younger, my little four-year-old piped up from the back of the car one day, 'Mummy, we're monsters, aren't we?'

In the puzzled silence that followed, my daughter suddenly said, 'No Caleb, we're not monsters, we're *aliens*!'

I recalled that a few days before, we'd read their favourite book of that moment about an alien who

visited earth from outer space. Trying to introduce a spiritual lesson from an ordinary story time I'd explained
that, because our real home is in heaven, Christians are a
bit like aliens on this earth.

His mistake made me chuckle, but the truth is that for
many in this world, we are actually perceived as monsters.

Listen to a discussion on the radio if you don't believe
me! Hear how a Christian who rings to give a biblical
perspective on a moral discussion is vilified. Watch how
Christians are portrayed as weird in TV dramas and
soaps. Read about fellow believers who are tortured,
imprisoned and even killed in Muslim and Communist
countries for nothing more than living for Christ.

Although Haman was the true monster, most
applauded him, as most people in Germany applauded
Hitler.

It's easy to fall into the trap of believing that everything is so much worse in our country than it's ever
been. Certainly there are growing restrictions on our religious liberties we wouldn't have dreamt of even a few
years ago and the moral climate has deteriorated signif-
icantly. Of course we need to pray and make a stand but
we also need to read our Bibles and a few history books
to remind ourselves that God's people have always suffered.

Peter is addressing a severely persecuted church when
he writes:

> Dear friends, don't be surprised by the fiery trials you are
> going through, as if something strange were happening to
> you. Instead be very glad—because these trials will make
> you partners with Christ in his suffering, and afterward
> you will have the wonderful joy of sharing his glory when
> it is displayed to all the world. (1 Pet. 4:12–13)

If we're surprised, we'll be shaken in our stand. If we take our eyes off Jesus suffering for us, we'll be disillusioned. If we take our eyes off future glory we'll lose heart.

But what does Peter mean when he instructs us to be *'very glad'*? How can that ever be possible?

A Tiny Glimmer of Hope

Even in the middle of this uproar there is a small glimmer of hope for God's people. It's found in chapter 3:

> In the twelfth year of King Xerxes, in the first month, the month of Nisan they cast the pur (that is a lot) in the presence of Haman to select a day and month and the lot fell on the twelfth month, the month of Adur. (3:7, NIV)

It was Passover time.

While Haman relied on superstition to determine the future, the Jews celebrated the reality of God's faithfulness in the past. As Haman contemplated extermination they remembered a great deliverance. As the dice fell to set a future date (in eleven months' time), God watched over his enemy's shoulders. He knew that by the time Passover came around again his people would be celebrating another great deliverance.

Samuel Rutherford the Scottish Puritan said in the seventeenth century, 'Christ chargeth me to believe his daylight at midnight.'[3] And that's the key to being 'very glad' as Peter put it!

It's looking back over our past deliverances with thankfulness and trusting God for the future. Why? Because that same God in our past is the same God in the future and he's been there already.

Joseph Hart summed this up in only two short verses of his most famous hymn:

> How good is the God we adore.
> Our faithful, unchangeable friend!
> His love is as great as his power.
> And knows neither measure nor end!
>
> 'Tis, Jesus, the first and the last,
> Whose spirit will guide us safe home,
> We'll praise him for all that is past,
> And trust him for all that's to come.[4]
>
> *Joseph Hart, 1712–68*

Questions for Personal Reflection

1. What are you feeling pressurised to conform to in your life at the moment?
2. Consider your reasons for not bowing to that pressure. Are they based on culture and tradition or do you have well reasoned arguments based on a biblical foundation?
3. John 15:18–21 tells us that if we follow Christ we will be persecuted. What are some scriptural strategies to help us stand firm? See Matt. 5:43–45; Rom. 12:14; Matt. 10:16; Matt. 10:17–20; Acts 5:29; Matt. 5:10–12.
4. Read through Haman's character traits again. Ask yourself honestly if any of these resemble you in any way? Does he remind you of areas in your life that you need to address?

Real Men Cry

☞ *Read ESTHER 4*

Faith isn't the first word that springs to mind as Mordecai's loud crying echoes down to us through the centuries. Despair, grief or anguish perhaps describe the scene more realistically. Has Mordecai's faith been chased away by tears?

Caroline Williams, a friend of mine, wrote these words after her ten-year-old daughter died: 'Don't assume that having faith takes away the pain; it can't, it just lifts your head above the clouds and says: LOOK UP!'

How would you define faith? Is it a kind of armour that protects us from pain? Is it a strait-jacket that restricts our feelings and emotions? A walking stick, that helps us to hobble along, despite our wounds? Is it false hope or wishful thinking?

Hebrews 11:1 defines faith for us: 'What is faith? It is the confident assurance that what we hope for is going to happen. It is the evidence of things we cannot yet see.'

John White stated: 'Faith is man's response to God's initiative.'[1]

And Linda Dillow writes:

God does not demand that you and I have blind faith, but abandoned faith, a faith that trusts him fully. Through his word, God willingly reveals much about who he is, what his plans are, and what he requires of us. As we come to see him and know him, he urges, 'TRUST ME.'[2]

The expression of our faith is multifaceted. Sometimes it involves skipping alongside our God, sometimes holding his hand in the darkness of a tunnel of which we can't yet see the end. Sometimes, it feels like we're gripping on to him by our very fingernails, while the storm seeks to rip us away from him, at others it's enjoying complete calm in the haven of his arms. Faith is that confident assurance that although our circumstances may change, and with them our emotions, he does not change and neither does his word.

I was greatly helped by a little phrase I heard in a sermon recently: Faith is not the same thing as serenity.

As we read through Esther chapter 4 and look at Mordecai's immediate reaction there isn't a lot of serenity – but there's a great deal of faith – and that faith affects him in many different ways throughout the chapter.

Faith permitted him to grieve

'When Mordecai learned what had been done, he tore his clothes, put on sackcloth and ashes, and went out into the city, crying with a loud and bitter wail.' (Esth. 4:1)

He was devastated. He couldn't have kept his upper lip stiff even if he'd tried. Emotion was a suitable response, and he wasn't ashamed to show it. As the news spread among the Jews, so an increasing cry of desolation echoed through the empire. Their plight was bewildering as well as desperate. Michele Guinness in her autobiography *Child of the Covenant* points out that 'Jews are often fiercely patriotic for their adopted homelands even though they are predominantly Jewish.'[3]

This threat was unreasonable, unjust and unexpected. They felt abandoned and powerless. Yet in their grief, they cried to the only one who could help them. God, whose glory was at stake.

This faith prohibited false guilt

How would you have felt if you'd been in Mordecai's shoes? I suspect that if I'd been him I'd have hidden or run away. Think about it for a minute. If you'd brought all this trouble on an entire nation wouldn't you have felt racked with guilt? But not Mordecai. He realized that this was bigger than a tiff between him and Haman. This was a satanic onslaught, and he didn't allow himself to be disabled by the lies and accusations of the devil.

John White writes in *The Fight*:

> Feelings of guilt will take the sparkle out of your eye and the snap out of your step. They will dull the edge of your witness, take the heart out of Christian service and make any public testimony as stale as moldy fish. And this is precisely what Satan has in mind. Accusation is his secret weapon, supremely effective in taking the zap out of the Christian army's attack. How could guilt-ridden soldiers, possibly assail the gates of hell?[4]

I understand what he's saying. There are two opponents I seem to spend a lot of time and energy combatting. The first is *fear* (something we'll look at later). The second is *false guilt*. Ever felt like this?

'I'm not committed enough in my job, I'm not as available as I should be for other women in my church, my house is too untidy, I'm not witnessing enough, I'm a useless wife, I've never played enough with my children or read them enough books, I'm wasting my time on this project, I don't pray enough.' The list is endless.

I feel guilty about not taking exercise and yet when I do go to the gym I feel I should be somewhere else doing something more worthwhile. I can even feel guilty about feeling guilty!

One friend told me she feels guilty because she's single. When I probed she said, 'I tell myself that if I'd chosen another profession or stuck with that guy I knew years ago or moved city, then perhaps I would have married.'

Another blames herself for her marriage break-up despite her spouse's serial adultery.

These conversations help highlight how destructive false guilt is. It's not the same as conviction. They lead us down two very different roads. Conviction is God's tool for drawing us to him. It directs us to Christ because full forgiveness is available. Conviction is actually part of the process of having our shame taken away! It gives us hope and leads us to joy! False guilt however is Satan's tool for driving us *away* from God. It leads only to despair. It's all about our failures and nothing about Christ's success on the cross.

It's vital we recognize the difference between the two. Faith enables us to refuse to allow those lies of Satan to take root.

Faith fuelled his passion

What is passion?

The Oxford Dictionary defines passion as: '1) strong emotion; 2) an outburst of anger; 3) intense sexual love;

4) a strong enthusiasm; 5) (the Passion) the suffering of Christ, during his last days.'[5]

Mordecai is not the only man with passion in the story of Esther. King Xerxes was passionate about:

- Power.
  His navy boasted a deadly reputation and were the most proficient in the world. One thousand hand-picked bodyguards known as the Immortals attended him personally with golden apples on their spear butts. His shock force of nine thousand carried silver apples on theirs. The historian Herodotus wrote that, 'If one of them were killed and fell sick, a replacement would immediately step forward to fill the gap in the ranks.' His cavalry comprised of the men from Persia and various subject nations. Although Persian propaganda exaggerated army numbers to cause fear and panic, most historians estimate he commanded around two hundred and fifty thousand men.
- Beauty.
- Luxury.
- Sex.
- Horticulture and hunting.
  The king was a keen gardener and horticulture rivalled hunting as a passion of the court. Most capitals had their own parks, not only stocked with game, but with lakes, streams, pavilions, manicured lawns and exotic plants, trees and flowers. There is a story that he once came across a plane tree, near Sardis, of such beauty that he halted his entire army to admire it. One of the Immortals was dispatched from his company and ordered to serve it as guard. Golden jewellery brought out from the expedition's mobile treasure trove was festooned from its sweeping branches.[6]

- Culture.
- Friends.

Haman was another passionate man. We've already seen his love of power, applause, revenge and a life without God and his people. We've seen that both these men were prone to strong emotion and outbursts of anger. Their passions were mainly 'me' centred.

But when it comes to Mordecai there is a different kind of passion. Look again at the fifth definition in the Oxford Dictionary of the Passion:

The suffering of Christ, during his last days.

'The Passion' isn't a biblical term and yet over the centuries has become a popular description of those final days leading right up to, and including, Christ's death. Whether or not we choose to use the term, it does remind us, that present within him there was a special kind of passion that drove him willingly and deliberately to the cross.

Christ, the promised Messiah, had passion for God's glory. He was passionate that men and women and children across the nations would know and experience that glory. He was passionate about God's people. He was passionate that they might believe. Christ was in no way 'me-centred', but 'God-centred' and 'other-centred'.

Christ alone showed the *ultimate* passion by bearing the full force of God's anger for our sin. Yet it was the same *type* of passion that faith fuelled in Mordecai. He too was passionate about God's glory, and God's people. So much so that he put his life on the line, by drawing attention to his Jewishness and approaching the court boundary. If Esther's servants noticed him it was very likely his enemies did too.

Faith propelled him to action, and in the right direction

'He stood outside the gate of the palace, for no one was allowed to enter while wearing clothes of mourning.' (Esth. 4:2)

Mordecai was not giving up hope. He didn't wait for someone else to take the lead. Neither did he bury his head in the sand and hope the problem would go away. He went back to the place where the trouble had started and where he believed it could end.

John White writes 'Faith is your decision to respond to God's word . . . In time the decision grows into an attitude, an attitude of always being ready to respond positively to God's word.'[7] Mordecai was ready again. Because he walked in faith, this next step came naturally to him.

Faith convinced him of the providence of God

He realized that God had ordained the crowning of Esther for this very reason, and this very time.

'Who can say but that you have been elevated to the palace for just such a time as this?' he asks her in verse 14. He marvelled at how God had planned so carefully for this very occasion. This threat was no surprise to God, who'd planned deliverance well in advance.

Faith reminded him of God's promises

At the beginning of verse 14, he says these startling words to Esther, 'If you keep quiet at a time like this, deliverance for the Jews *will* arise from some other place' (emphasis mine). Although he grieved and feared for the future he remained confident that even if many died, Israel *would not* be exterminated. God had promised a hope, and a future: God had promised the Messiah through the line of David.

Faith encouraged him to expect great things of Esther

Mordecai wasn't content for Esther to live a sheltered life in a place where no one would suspect her of being a Jew. 'Surely the palace is the last place anyone will look?' he could have reasoned. Not at all! He expected her to be a 'difference-maker' even if that put her life at risk. He believed that God had equipped her with everything she needed to make an impact. He demanded that she follow his example of courageous leadership. He believed that refusal wasn't an option and that disobedience would have been a sin.

Consider whether you would have desired this same level of commitment from *your* child? *Do* you long that your child will be a 'difference-maker', whatever the cost for them in terms of popularity and worldly affirmation? If the time were to come when to follow Christ would (as in so many parts of the world) mean putting the lives of our families at risk, could you do it?

If we ourselves have Mordecai's firm grasp of God's holiness and glory in one hand and the seriousness and bitter consequences of sin in the other, surely we will make every effort to train our children in a direction that aligns with God's word. We will recognize that ultimately, only a fully obedient lifestyle will bring glory to him and true blessing to them.

Esther's happiness and human success wasn't the most important thing to Mordecai – he cared more about her eternal future.

Faith warned him that we are all accountable to God

'If you keep quiet at a time like this . . . you and your relatives will die.' (Esth.4:14)

How was that for straight talking? He understood he would not be able to cover up for her or protect her from judgment. He warned her of the consequences . . . why? Because he cared. He'd always been tender towards her, but now he proved his tenderness, by his toughness.

A few months ago, my husband Wes preached the most difficult sermon of his life, a complete sermon on God's judgement and hell. He felt overwhelmed by the seriousness of it in both his preparation and delivery. He feared that those who appeared to be searching for God would be turned off by the harshness of the subject. I, who knew what was coming next, kept resisting the urge to stick my fingers in my ears. He never raised his voice: yet it was a powerful sermon with a terrifying message.

So why preach it? Because it was the loving thing to do. True Christian love means a willingness to warn of the consequences of disobedience just as Christ challenged and warned throughout his ministry.

C. S. Lewis wrote 'Christianity is hard as nails, hard and tender at the same time. It's the blend that does it; neither quality would be good without the other' and also 'Love is something more stern and splendid than mere kindness.'[8]

Faith enabled him to rest

'So Mordecai went away and did as Esther told him.' (4:17) He'd done all he could for now, apart from rallying the Jews to prayer and fasting. Now, it was in God's hands. He settled down to pray for wisdom and courage for Esther and for God's deliverance.

Faith prevented him from fearing

If we skip ahead to the next chapter, we find Mordecai at the gate three days later. As Haman passes by 'he saw Mordecai sitting at the gate, not standing up or trembling before him' (5:9).

This is where we see faith and serenity walking together.

Mordecai's actions are pretty amazing, don't you think, considering all that's happened? How did he stay on his feet? The secret is that Mordecai feared God and that prevented him fearing even this monster. He was assured that his future was in God's hands not in Haman's. He didn't fear man because he didn't fear death.

He could say with Martin Luther (the fifteenth-century theologian who inspired the Reformation despite much personal danger and conflict) 'Here I stand, I can do no other.'

A Hero of Faith

The British are not known for hero worship. We love to support the underdog, on the rise to success and celebrity status, but once they've made it, we start the campaign of criticism and dethronement. We see this illustrated daily in the newspapers. It completely baffles me that any man in his right mind would want to be the England football manager. Heroes only seem to become true heroes when they're dead, and they can't do any more to blot their copybook. The first and second commandments tell us that only God is to be worshipped, but surely we need heroes of our Christian faith? Not to worship but to inspire us?

Jim Elliot, despite the threat of many dangers, went as a missionary to the Auca people in Ecuador. He and four colleagues were martyred with wooden spears. In *The Mark of a Man*, Jim Elliot's widow, Elisabeth, comments that although many admit to how he has inspired them, these same people are often careful not to be seen as putting him on a pedestal or viewing him as a hero. She asks:

> Well, what is a hero, anyway? Any man admired for his courage, nobility, or exploits, the central figure in any important event, honoured for outstanding qualities.
>
> Wasn't Jim, a hero? We badly need heroes. How else shall we grasp the meaning of courage or strength or holiness? We need to see such truth made visible in the lives of human beings, and Jim did that, it seems to me.[9]

Mordecai is a genuine hero of faith. He shows us what strength, courage and purity looks like. Let's learn from him.

Questions for Personal Reflection

1. A friend whose world seemed to be crumbling around her commented, 'I'm struggling with my faith. How can I have faith in the future when the past has brought me to where I am now?' Using Mordecai's faith as a bench-mark, how would you answer her?

2. How can we recognize the difference between conviction and false guilt? What strategy can we employ to combat Satan's lies? See Phil. 3:13–14; 2 Cor. 10:5; Eph. 2:8.

3. Make a list of the things you feel passionately about. Now number them in order of priority.

4. 'What's more, who can say but that you have been elevated to the palace for just such a time as this?' Meditate on this verse, contemplating your own life, circumstances and opportunities. Ask God to use you in this place for such a time as this.

The Emergence of a Queen

☞ *Re-read ESTHER 4*

If a pupa could think and feel, I wonder what would run through its mind. Would it relive its laborious caterpillar days, as it hauled itself over leaf after leaf? Would it wonder what life is all about? Would its eyes search the darkness of its prison and feel loneliness and despair? As the time approaches to break free, would it experience fear and doubt about the future? Perhaps, as it stretches out its wings and enjoys that very first flight of freedom, it admires what it has become and breathes, 'Oh . . . so that's what it was all about!'

Esther's life reminds me of the life cycle of a butterfly. There seems to be three stages of it recorded in the Book of Esther.

1) The Price of Preparation

> The life of a caterpillar is far from glamorous. It
> spends almost all its time either eating or shedding
> its skin. It expands in size until its new skin
> hardens, then it anchors itself to a stem and
> prepares to change into a chrysalis.

Esther's early life had been a tough one. It needed to be.
God was preparing her for an even greater challenge.

Do you remember the story of David before he went
to fight Goliath? For days, the Philistines had threatened
and mocked the strongest of Israel's warriors. They all
shook before him but young David insisted to King Saul:

> I have been taking care of my father's sheep . . . When a lion
> or a bear comes to steal a lamb from the flock, I go after it
> with a club and take the lamb from its mouth. If the animal
> turns on me, I catch it by the jaw and club it to death. I have
> done this to both lions and bears, and I'll do it to this pagan
> Philistine too, for he has defied the armies of the living God!
> The LORD who saved me from the claws of the lion and the
> bear will save me from this Philistine! (1 Sam. 17: 34–37)

David did not come to this battle, cold and inexperi-
enced. He'd been facing giants (albeit four-legged ones)
for years! As a shepherd he was being prepared for
kingship and the job of shepherding God's people. It
seemed a pretty unlikely preparation route, but God's
way was more effective than any onlooker could have
predicted. Esther didn't immediately share David's confidence in the battle ahead. But Mordecai did. He recognized that her experiences up to this point had proven

her potential. He also had every confidence in God's delivering power and he encouraged her to have confidence too.

Let's remind ourselves of her life so far.

- Born in exile.
- Orphaned in childhood.
- Adopted.
- Disappointed dreams. There was to be no loving companion or normal family life for her.
- The forced separation from those she loved.
- Imprisonment with strangers.
- Cultural and social re-education, much of which was likely to have been unwelcome.
- A sexual encounter with a stranger, who held her life in his hands.
- The bewilderment of a sex and beauty contest victory.
- Intense public interest and scrutiny.
- Marriage to a difficult, remote and unpredictable man, who was far from monogamous.
- An unusual home life with no true intimacy.

As I ponder Esther's life up to now, I have to wonder how I would have coped with all this tragedy.

Trials either make us bitter, or they make us better. Esther showed no sign of bitterness, but she certainly became better.

James writes, 'For when your faith is tested, your endurance has a chance to grow. So let it grow, for when your endurance is fully developed, you will be strong in character and ready for anything.' (Jas. 1: 3–4)

And Corrie Ten Boon once wisely said 'I've learned that we must hold everything loosely, because when I grip it tightly, it hurts when my Father pries my fingers loose and takes it from me.'[1]

This was a lesson Esther had been taught from an early age.

2) The Time for Transformation

> The pupa stage is often called the resting stage. But inside it's hard skin, the creature is undergoing an amazing transformation controlled by its chemical hormones.

We don't know much of the five-year time slot, between Esther's coronation and Mordecai 's appeal to her, but there are strong indications of her transformation from a mere queen to respected leader.

In 1975, Dr James Dobson wrote a book that he bravely entitled *What Wives Wish Their Husbands Knew about Women* (known as *Man to Man about Women* in the UK).[2] It must be a hot topic because more than thirty years later it's still in print and over 2 million copies have been sold! Peter seriously recognized this highly significant principle of marriage when he wrote to husbands: 'Treat her with understanding as you live together.' (1 Pet. 3:7)

In other words, 'Get to know your wife on the inside as well as the outside! Discover *who* she is, not simply *what* she is!' Five years into marriage and Esther is terrified to approach her husband. (See 2:16 and 3:7 for timescale). He doesn't seem to know her in anything other than a physical sense. He is ignorant of her background and all the aspects of her life that have made her her. He hasn't even made the effort to commission his private detectives to discover her nationality.

I suspect there weren't any leisurely chats over breakfast in bed or many romantic dinners or walks in the park. No weekends away, and little physical appreciation or contact without sex. They didn't even live together during the week. Yet isn't the Bible wonderful? It gives us the perfect model for our lives, but through its characters relates to normal, hurting people.

Chapters 1 to 3 of Genesis outline the model of God's plan for marriage but Esther would be in a position to sympathize with those of us who find ourselves in situations and relationships that are far from that ideal, because of sin. If she were here, Esther would be able to relate to the lonely, those who long for a soul mate and wives who are materially pampered yet emotionally starved. She would understand the challenges of living with a man with a different faith or no faith at all. She would empathize with those who know fear of an uncertain future or those who feel the physical pressure of always being beautiful, of always being on hand to bring sexual gratification. She would be familiar with the husband who's completely wrapped up in his own career, interests and power. And she would relate to that dread of sleeping with a man who you suspect is comparing you with other women.

Yet I believe Esther would do more than simply sympathize. Her response to her circumstances challenges us. Unbelievable as it may seem, there is no evidence to suggest that she allowed self-pity to get a foothold in her life or that she took any of her misery out on those around her. It's doubtful she could afford the luxury of introspection. Rather the evidence in chapter 4 points to the fact that while she was continually beautified on the outside by an army of beauticians, she persevered in the cultivation of her inner beauty. Peter wrote:

> In the same way, you wives must accept the authority of your husbands, even those who refuse to accept the Good News. Your godly lives will speak to them better

than any words. They will be won over by watching your pure, godly behavior.

Don't be concerned about the outward beauty that depends on fancy hairstyles, expensive jewelry, or beautiful clothes. You should be known for the beauty that comes from within, the unfading beauty of the gentle and quiet spirit, which is so precious to God. That is the way the holy women of old made themselves beautiful. They trusted God and accepted the authority of their husbands. For instance, Sarah obeyed her husband, Abraham, when she called him her master. You are her daughters when you do what is right, without fear of what your husbands might do. (1 Pet. 3: 1–6)

This wife knew the reality of living with a man who refused to acknowledge God. Ultimately, she did win him over in the battle for the survival of the Jews and the promised Christ, who meant good news for us all. Vashti's technique of confronting the king had not worked even if her motives had been correct. Yet for Esther, her respect and submission to her husband and the development of a gentle and quiet spirit helped to turn this whole event around.

Let's look a little deeper at that passage in 1 Peter quoted above, and how Esther, like Sarah, is a living example of Peter's command. It outlines the characteristics of inner beauty.

- Purity and godliness.
- Submission to husband.
- Gentleness and quietness.
- Trust in God.
- Absence of fear.

Not exactly the world's perspective of beauty! Yet it's a wise choice from every other perspective.

1) *The eternal perspective*

Outward beauty fades, inward beauty grows.

Outward beauty is for the here and now, inward beauty is for the future.

Outward beauty focuses attention on ourselves, inward beauty points to God.

Outward beauty dies, inward beauty lives forever.

Taking time to become the women God desires us to be is recognition that life on earth is a preparation for Heaven.

2) *The historical perspective*

This passage is not just a New Testament principle. It tells us that holy women, right through the ages, understood this secret of true beauty. Their role model was Sarah from way back in Genesis. Peter brings this principle alive and tells us to carefully study the lives of Sarah, and other women in the Bible and church history. He's confident that if we do we'll covet their way of living.

3) *God's perspective on us*

Esther might have doubted her value to Xerxes in anything other than her outward beauty. But to her heavenly Father, her inner beauty was precious.

Our value is truly measured by our Creator. His scales are far more accurate than those of our parents, friends, husbands or children. In fact, we are so highly prized by him that he sent his son – he that was most precious to him – to die on a cross for us. There he carried our sin, our judgment and our shame. Our worth to him is not dependent on our circumstances, or our role in life. Nor is it based on how much we please him. There isn't a thing we can do to increase or decrease his love for us. We are precious, because we are precious! That's Grace! That's security!

When I ponder this truth my heart is flooded with joy, thanksgiving and freedom. It cleanses my conscience and reminds me I am clean. It makes me ask 'What can I do for him in response to this? How can I thank him?'

Despite not looking like a Hollywood star, every morning I make a choice. Shall I enhance what beauty I possess or not? Most days I make the effort, so I shower, style my hair, apply some make-up and endeavour to select some clothes that match. Taking exercise, eating well and drinking that daily two litres of water take a lot more discipline yet long-term, are much more important than the surface enhancement.

But even more importantly, Peter recognizes that the enhancement of *inner* beauty is precious to God. When we devote ourselves to purity, he rejoices. When we determine to mirror Christ's submission to his father, he delights.

If this is God's perspective of us, doesn't it automatically follow that he wants what's best for us? He knows this attitude, even of submission to an unbelieving husband, makes sense. It is far more likely to disarm him and defuse a difficult situation. As we glorify God through obedience to him we will have the peace of a clear conscience.

God gives husbands their own responsibilities in marriage, and he's angry when they fail to love and lead their wives, as they should. But they alone are accountable to God for their behaviour. In other words, I am not responsible for my husband's side of the relationship but I am fully responsible for mine.

Submission in our society is wrongly misunderstood as weakness. Yet biblical submission is voluntary and willing and an acknowledgement that God created our husbands to lead us – even if they are unbelievers. We have Jesus as our ultimate role model in this. None of us would consider *him* weak, for submitting to the Father to die for us, would we?

You might say that Esther *had* to submit to Xerxes because he was the king. You might argue that she lived in terror the whole of her married life. For us, there are biblical exceptions for divorce. None of us are required to stay in marriages where they apply. For Esther, no such option was available.

Yet, I think she *willingly* submitted. Submission indicates strength of character. If she'd been downtrodden and squashed, she would have been timid with those around her. Isn't it usually the case that a woman who views herself as a 'victim' is vulnerable to others as well? The woman we've looked at in the palace was certainly not downtrodden. She was not a victim. God evidently provided what she lacked in affection from Xerxes. Perhaps she rejoiced in Isaiah's words: 'for your creator will be your husband. The LORD Almighty is his name! He is your Redeemer, the Holy One of Israel, the God of all the earth.' (Is. 54:5)

4) A right perspective on God

As we trust in God's sovereignty, we will submit without fear of the mistakes our husbands might make, or the possible consequences of living a pure life. We recognize that God holds our future in his hands. Sarah is an interesting choice as an example, carted around the land and because of Abraham's lies of self-protection was put into moral danger by rulers – not once, but twice! (Gen. 12 and 20)

5) A perspective on God, through us, that is attractive

All of us are works in progress and none of us will attain perfection until we reach heaven. But despite our failings

Peter assures us that if our perspectives are right then those around us *will* see God in us.

The general tone of our lives will be marked by gentleness, humility and self-control in both our actions and reactions. There will be a strength and assurance that can't fail to have an effect on others.

As Proverbs 31:30 tells us, 'Charm is deceptive, and beauty does not last; but a woman who fears the LORD will be greatly praised.' We might even win our husbands over to the Lord.

There is clear evidence in chapter 5 that Esther had cultivated that beauty within.

- She remained loyal to her adopted father. Back in Esther 2:22, rather than furthering her own position with the king, she gave credit where credit was due.
- Esther continued to accept the wise advice of Mordecai.
- She had built good relationships with her staff. She had not allowed power to go to her head. Her maids and eunuchs passed on the message about Mordecai's distress. She had faith in Hathach, trusting him to honestly serve her by being her messenger. Mordecai followed her lead and likewise trusted him to convey the whole story to her.
- She wasn't insipid but had grown in authority. She gave an order to her servants, and it was followed: 'She ordered him [Hathach] to go to Mordecai and find out what was troubling him . . .' (Esth.4:5b)

By the end of this chapter, she is issuing the command not only to Mordecai himself, but also to all the Jews in Suza. Her time in the palace has not been wasted. She's used her circumstances well to grow her character.

3) Freedom for the flight

After several weeks, the skin of the pupa splits and the adult butterfly emerges. Blood pumps into the wing veins to expand them, and the damp crumpled wings soon spread and dry.

The day that Esther needed to fly did not start well. Something was dreadfully wrong and what made it worse was that she didn't know what.

Esther 4:4 tells us she was deeply distressed. When Mordecai refused to replace his sackcloth with the clothes she sent him (perhaps so he could enter the palace gate, where she could speak to him directly) her sense of urgency increased, and she sent Hathach, who was both the king's eunuch and her attendant, to find out what was wrong. There could be no mistake in the reply: Mordecai gave too many details for the report to be dismissed as rumour. He even had a copy of the actual death warrant for all Jews.

Esther's distress soon heightened to panic and denial at the suggestion that she was the one to beg for mercy and plead for her people. She was terrified to obey his request on three fronts.

1. Court etiquette was designed to protect the king's life from would-be assassins. The practice was that the king would extend his gold sceptre only to one whom he knew and from whom he welcomed a visit.
2. For 30 days Esther had not been called for. This was obviously of concern to her. Perhaps she was worried in case she was out of favour, or about to be replaced as Queen Vashti had been.

3. Nehemiah tells how during the reign of Xerxes' son, he deliberately came before the king with a sad face. 'I had never appeared sad in his presence before this time. So the king asked me, "Why are you so sad? You aren't sick, are you? You look like a man with deep troubles." Then, I was badly frightened . . .' (Neh. 2:1b–2)

Sadness, in the king's presence, was a dangerous emotion to display. It conveyed displeasure in the way the king governed. That was why Mordecai's 'mourning suit' had prevented him from entering the palace gate. Yet this is *exactly* what he asked Esther to do – to go to the king, not only without an invitation but also in distress.

Cocooned in her royal quarters, she had been completely oblivious to the uproar around her. She'd had no warning of this, no time to prepare a plan or see for herself her responsibility. This was a bolt out of the blue. No wonder she trembled.

I heard of a woman who remembered her mother's words to her each night as she was tucked up in bed from the age of four. 'You are here for God and for other people. The world is waiting for you!'

What an amazing perception of life to instil into a child or an adult! 'You are here for God and for other people.'

In a nutshell, this is similar to what Mordecai says to Esther. 'Esther – you're not a queen for yourself and your own comfort and protection. Ultimately, you are not simply here for your husband the king. No – you're here for God and for other people.'

> Don't think for a moment that you will escape there in the palace when all other Jews are killed. If you keep quiet at a time like this, deliverance for the Jews will arise from some

other place, but you and your relatives will die. What's more, who can say that you have been elevated to the palace for just such a time as this? (Esth. 4: 13–14)

Good theology cannot be watered down. If it is, God's word ceases to change our lives. Mordecai did not challenge Esther with a simply emotional appeal. Nor was he exerting unfair pressure or blackmailing her. Rather, he appealed to her with the sound theology of God's sovereignty and her responsibility.

1. God's sovereignty. He told her that God is firmly in control. He will deliver his people, whatever method he chooses and whoever he uses. He challenged her to consider God's sovereignty, in putting her in the exalted position she finds herself. 'Come on Esther! Think about it! Could this be what it's all been about?'
2. Esther's responsibility. Mordecai shows her that God isn't asking her to be successful, but he does demand faithfulness. Deliverance is in God's hands, but obedience is in hers, and she will be held accountable for that.

That's the key to unlocking the chains of fear.

When she realizes that the result is in God's hands, not hers, she is free to fly. When she rests in this sovereignty, courage is hers. As she looks to God, resolve replaces defeat.

We know she looks to him because she appeals for prayer and devotes herself to the same. Perhaps, what she had considered a hindrance (not being called to the king in such a long time) was actually a blessing as it drove her to reliance on God, rather than on her own position and resourcefulness.

'Go and gather together all the Jews of Susa and fast for me. Do not eat or drink for three days, night and day. My maids and I will do the same.' (4:16a).

Notice how authoritative she is! Can this be the same Esther as only a few minutes ago?

One unusual thing strikes me in this verse. She not only promises her own serious prayer and fasting, but also her maids. Now, who were these maids? There's no indication that they were sister Jewesses, yet she expected their spiritual devotion in this matter. I wonder if these women were further evidence of Esther's godly example and influence on those around her in the palace. Perhaps they had become worshippers of the true God of Israel.

'And then, though it is against the law, I will go to see the king. If I must die, I am willing to die.' (4:16b)

Esther had very quickly developed an eternal perspective. She had been confined so far by the laws around her, but now realizes that where state is pitched against God, then it is God who must be followed. If it is living a life of compromise and denial of her Lord, or death, then it must be death.

Anne Askew repeatedly refused to deny her faith, believing that the Bible was the word of God, rather than the traditions of the Roman Catholic faith. Despite being tortured on the rack to the extent that she never walked again, she asserted 'I would rather die than break my faith.' She had to be carried on a chair to the stake at Smithfield, by her fellow martyrs on 16 July 1546. Resolutely ignoring release papers brought even at the last moment, she chose to burn.[3]

Her body might have been chained and broken, but her soul was free even before the flames consumed her. She recognized her treasure was in heaven, not on this earth.

Horatio G. Spafford wrote around three hundred years later:

For me it is Christ, it is Christ now to live!
Though deaths waters over me roll,
No fear shall be mine, for in death as in life.
You will whisper your peace to my soul,
It is well, it is well with my soul.
But, Lord, for your coming in glory, we wait;
The sky, not the grave is our goal;
The trumpet shall sound and the Lord shall
    descend:
Bless the Lord, bless the Lord, oh, my soul!

It is well, it is well with my soul.[4]

Esther's people were waiting for Christ to come for the first time, not the second; they knew he was coming and that changed their perspective on everything.

After years of music making, K.T. Tunstall was finally recognized as Best British Female Solo artist at the 2006 Brit Awards. Before she left the stage, she triumphantly raised her trophy and shouted 'Ladies! Disregard your limits!'

This was undoubtedly a battle cry for feminism but Esther was certainly not a feminist. However she disregarded her limits, and they were many, ultimately, even disregarding the limit and possibility of her death.

So ladies, what are the limits you need to disregard in order to live the life God has called you to? Is it your past? Are you ashamed of where you came from and what you've become? Is it your present role? Do you long to be married? To have children? To be well? To be loved? Is it a fear for the future? Of what standing up for God will entail? It's crucial that we too, like Esther, grasp God's sovereignty.

Linda Dillow writes:

Remember, God is the Blessed Controller of all things (1 Timothy 6:15). He has assigned us our portion and our cup (Psalm 16:5). God is in control of all the uncontrollables in our lives: What we can't see, what doesn't make sense to us, and what we don't understand . . . There are no accidents, no mistakes, no miscalculations. All is under His sovereign control, and nothing is permitted but what He has decreed. And what He has decreed is intended for our good and for His glory. His absolute sovereignty means that I can trust Him with my tiniest doubt or with my most heart-wrenching fear. Knowing that God is in control makes trusting Him easier. It also helps to know that He is wise.[5]

Questions for Personal Reflection

1. List the past events and circumstances of your life that have contributed to where you are and what you're doing now. Highlight which ones have strengthened you in your faith and any which have knocked you off course. Do you feel bitter about any of them? What does Hebrews 12:15 warn us about

2. How does the inner beauty identified by Peter in 1 Peter 3:1–6 make sense not only to married women but to all women, single, divorced or widowed? See 1 Peter 3: 8–12. How can you cultivate it in practical terms?

3. How will a proper understanding of God being the blessed controller of all things transform your life at this moment?

Lonely, but not Alone

☞ *Read ESTHER 5:1–8*

The Oxford Dictionary defines courage as 'the ability to disregard one's fear.'[1] The wife of American evangelist, Dwight L. Moody, perfectly illustrates this ability through an amazing but terrifying ordeal while in Britain:

> Emma, travelling alone by train, entered what she supposed an empty compartment in which someone had left a bundle of old clothes. The train started. Out of the bundle a man's voice said, 'Do you know what I would have done with my wives if I had been Henry the Eighth?' He slid across to her side, leering. No trains had corridors in the 1860s. The next stop lay twenty minutes on.
>
> Emma, un-rattled always, merely said, 'No, do tell me.' The maniac recited bloodcurdling details, with strong hints that he intended to test his theories on her. When he paused to enjoy the effect of his words, she briskly said she knew better ways of execution, and each time he suggested a horror she capped it, keeping him still and absorbed until the train stopped and she escaped.[2]

Well, Esther was the wife of a king even more fearful than Henry VIII, and there wasn't a stop she could jump out at in twenty minutes either. She certainly needed courage and a plan. Lacking both, she appealed for help.

We saw in the last chapter how she called on Mordecai to mobilise the Jews in Suza to fast for three days. She and her maids did the same. Although she mentions fasting we can safely presume that this involved praying too.

'Three days later' (5:1) sound like three very insignificant words, don't they? In fact, they are of vital importance to the whole outcome of the events that follow. These were the days when the battle was actually won.

Charles Swindoll notes 'Living out the kingdom life means that everything must remain before the throne and under the authority of the ruler.'[3]

When Esther set out on this challenge of a lifetime, she recognized that although she was queen to Xerxes, there was one who sat on a higher throne and ruled with greater authority. She determined to submit all to him. Prayer was her priority. God was the focus.

I would love to have heard her prayers. Sometime ago there was an advertisement for British Telecom that asked 'Who would you most like to have a 1-2-1 with?' I'd choose Esther, and I'd ask her, 'How did you pray over those three days?'

One day perhaps, I'll get the opportunity, but until then, I can only surmise. It's pretty obvious that she pleaded, not only for her life, but also for the lives of others in her nation. I bet too, that she clung to God's promises and praised him for how he'd proved himself to her again and again. And if I'd been her I hope I'd have pondered all the ways he'd prepared me up to this point.

She had absolutely nowhere else to go, no one else to ask. We've already noted that she feared she was out of favour with the king. But it's a different Esther who emerges from her apartment three days later. Something has happened to her, the evidence of which is produced in the subsequent story. She has quite obviously met with God. As she enters the inner court with a plan in keeping with God's providence, her heart is guarded with God's peace and presence.

God's Peace and Presence

One day, while struggling to write a sympathy card to a friend, I asked my husband Wes what he would write. He said, 'That you're praying for God's peace and presence to be with her.' I've never thought of anything more appropriate since.

What else can we pray for, that is more necessary, not only for others, but also for ourselves? Whatever we're facing, from a day in hospital, to a mound of paperwork, God's peace and presence is what we need. The two are inextricably linked. To know God's presence is to know his peace. When we say, 'I want God's peace' it's usually because we *feel* that he's far away from our situation (notice I say ' feel'). When his peace floods our hearts, we *know* he's alongside us.

Most of us will be familiar with the verses in Philippians:

> Don't worry about anything; instead, pray about everything. Tell God what you need, and thank him for all he has done. If you do this, you will experience God's peace, which is far more wonderful than the human mind can understand. His peace will guard your hearts and minds as you live in Christ Jesus. (Phil. 4:6–7)

But this peace wasn't just promised for post-Pentecost Christians who've been left the Holy Spirit. Isaiah praises God, thus reminding him of this promise, 'You will keep in perfect peace all who trust in you, whose thoughts are fixed on you!' (Is. 26:3–4)

As Esther fixed her thoughts on God, through these three days of fasting and praying, God gave her perfect peace. It wasn't short-lived. It enabled her to be calm in the king's presence and to hold her nerve during the days ahead. As she passed before the king's Immortals (bodyguards), she walked with confidence, knowing the only true Immortal and Invisible God guarded her heart. Unless he willed it, no one could touch her.

Although Esther was alone in a very physical sense, she had the best kind of support. Paul instructs Timothy to, 'Pursue faith and love and peace, and enjoy the companionship of those who call on the Lord with pure hearts.' (2 Tim. 2:22b). What a brilliant phrase! '. . . enjoy the companionship of those who call on the Lord with pure hearts.'

Darlene Deibler Rose spent four years in a Japanese Prisoner of War Camp. She writes of the evening she'd been told of her husband's death:

> When I stretched out face down on my mat, I wanted nothing so much as a shoulder on which to put my aching head, and to sob until the fountain of my tears ran dry. I felt vulnerable and young, desperately needing the strong, comforting arm of the Shepherd. Who can bruise and make whole again? Who can break, then restore that which is shattered to a thing of beauty? . . . From force of habit, I "spread it out before the Lord." Never once did He interrupt while I told Him everything about the past, the present, the timing, what I was feeling—or not feeling—how the future looked, and the oppressive feeling

of aloneness. I waited to hear what my Lord would say and silence answered me. How unusually quiet it was in the barracks that night. Then like seeing clearly for the first time what the Artist had in mind, I understood— these people shared my grief. By their very quietness they were saying, "We're thinking of you and praying for you in your time of sorrow". Their words of sympathy, their tears, the warm pressure of their handclasps were the delicate shadings of empathy mingled with the warm hues of love to create upon the canvas of my heart a beautiful picture of friendship.[4]

Have you ever been going through an ordeal, and you're conscious that others are praying for you? Have you felt this kind of companionship?

The apostle Paul understood the value of the prayers of his brothers and sisters and made very specific prayer requests of those far away.

> Finally, dear brothers and sisters, I ask you to pray for us. Pray just that the Lord's message will spread rapidly and be honoured, wherever it goes, just as when it came to you. Pray, too, that we will be saved from wicked and evil people, for not everyone believes in the Lord. (2 Thes. 3:1–2)
>
> Pray for us, for our conscience is clear, and we want to live honorably in everything we do. I especially need your prayers right now so that I can come back to you soon. (Heb. 13:18–19)

If Paul and Esther realized the importance of the corporate and individual prayer, shouldn't we? Not only in requesting prayers for ourselves, but also as we plead for others.

Armed with God's peace and presence, Esther found courage, as his plan was revealed to her.

A plan that fitted perfectly with God's providence

Another question I'd like to ask Esther is, 'How did you come up with your idea?' It's so breathtakingly simple yet fits so exquisitely with God's plan that when you read chapter 5 and 6 it's almost impossible to separate God's action and Esther's. They move as one.

What impresses me about this woman is that even though she is deserving of our praise and respect, the greater glory always goes to God. She's so unassuming. She doesn't launch into an impassioned speech, or use flattery or seduction. Her plan is honest and straightforward. It allows her to be herself, and God to be God.

Although she disregarded the limits of fear, and even death, she regarded the limits of her position as resources. In other words, she saw what she had and allowed God to help her use them.

At the age of seventeen, Joni Eareckson broke her neck while diving, leaving her paralysed from the neck down. This was devastating for a young woman who loved sports, horse riding and art. Yet she describes the limits of her wheelchair as a tool.[5] She learnt to paint with her mouth and sing God's praises with her tongue, and she used her spiritual and physical experiences to encourage and challenge thousands of people across the world, both able-bodied and those who experience huge physical suffering, with the love of Christ.

Fear makes us negative. Fear causes us to concentrate on our limitations. For Esther those limitations were her sex, her position and her nationality, all rolled into one massive problem! The last time a woman stood up to the king, she was banished and chauvinism had become even more fashionable. What chance did she stand? She hadn't been flavour of the month, so why should the king take any notice of her? He'd been ruthless with

Vashti, why not more so with her when he discovers her background?

Faith makes us positive. Through her faith, Esther saw the opportunities. She remembered she was queen, embraced her position and made good use of all her resources.

Her resources:

- Her wardrobe and appearance. 'Esther put on her royal robes' (v. 1a). She took care how she dressed, appearing in clothes appropriate for the occasion. She looked like the queen and her beauty would have been enhanced.
- Access. '. . . and entered the inner court of the palace, just across from the king's hall.' (v. 1a) No one challenged her; after all, she was the queen. She would have walked with dignity in her robes, causing no alarm.
- An understanding of etiquette and culture. 'The king was sitting on his royal throne, facing the entrance. When he saw Queen Esther standing there in the inner court, he welcomed her, holding out the gold scepter to her. So Esther approached and touched its tip.' (vv. 1b–2) She didn't race into the throne room throwing herself at his feet dishevelled and tearstained. She waited until invited and approached with decorum.
- Initiative. 'When he saw Queen Esther...he welcomed her.' (v. 2) It was now 33 days since he'd last seen her in, but she appeared like a vision, before his eyes. He lost interest in whatever he was doing at the time and called her in. Perhaps he'd forgotten how beautiful she was and was flattered that this woman had come to him.
- The generosity of her husband. 'Then the king asked her, "What do you want, Queen Esther? What is your

request? I will give it to you, even if it is half the king-dom!' (v. 3) Xerxes was generous to those who pleased him and he was genuinely pleased with Esther. 'Half the kingdom' would have been an exaggerated state-ment, which wasn't meant to be taken literally (as with Herod's words to his stepdaughter in Mark 6:22–23) yet it indicated a genuine desire to lavish a gift upon her.

- Her home. 'And Esther replied, "If it please your Majesty, let the king and Haman come today to a ban-quet I have prepared for the king.' (v. 4) The king loved a good meal with a glass (or two) of quality wine. The fact he was free to go at such short notice is either an indication of a tedious day in the throne room or further evidence of Esther's wise timing.

- Haman's ambition. Esther even used Haman's lethal love of climbing the social ladder as a tool. 'The king turned to his attendants and said, "Tell Haman to come quickly to a banquet, as Esther has requested." So the king and Haman went to Esther's banquet.' (v. 5)

- Her secret identity. Do you see the humour of this book, even in the darkest of times and the most seri-ous situations? In verse 12, after Haman has bragged of his achievements to his friends and family he adds, 'And that's not all! Queen Esther invited only me and the king himself to the banquet she prepared for us. And she has invited me to dine with her and the King again tomorrow!' If only he'd known who she was! But he didn't, and she used this to her advantage.

- Her ability to entertain well. Her company and menu were so appreciated that Xerxes again asked what her request was, repeating the offer he'd made earlier that day. 'Esther replied, "This is my request and deepest wish. If Your Majesty is pleased with me and wants to grant my request, please come with Haman tomorrow to the banquet I will prepare for you.' (v. 7) 'What a happy man Haman was, as he left the banquet!' (v. 9a) He'd obviously had a thoroughly good time

- Patience. 'Then tomorrow I will explain what this is all about.' (v. 8b) Her heartaches and years of palace living had taught her to wait. She'd learned her lesson well. Esther held her nerve; she didn't blurt it all out, but waited, until the time was right. She reeled both men in, disarming them both with intrigue and suspense.
- Honesty. When it comes to the crunch of revealing all in chapter 7, no one questions or doubts her integrity. She is completely believed – we'll look at that later.
- God's provision and presence. Of course, he himself was her most powerful resource, and he was far from finished in his provision. As Esther faithfully pushed each door, God allowed them to swing open, with perfect precision.

He ensured that the diaries of both King and Prime Minister were empty. No political crisis stole their attention away. He opened the king's heart in generosity and warmth and provided an atmosphere in Esther's home of comfort and enjoyment. The meal didn't burn, and in a hundred tiny insignificant ways we can be sure that Esther would have been convinced she was not alone. I wonder if she was familiar with the Proverb that most of us know so well, 'Trust in the LORD with all your heart; do not depend on your own understanding. Seek his will in all you do, and he will direct your paths.' (Prov. 3:5)

Esther is proof that both this principle and promise is 100 per cent true.

Questions for Personal Reflection

1. List the aspects of your life that you perceive as a hindrance to your service to God.
2. List your opportunities and resources. How can some of the things you perceive as a hindrance actually be a tool in God's work?
3. Consider the occasions when fear stops you from being obedient.
4. Reflect on any times when prayer and/or fasting have resulted in courage, peace and the strength to choose the right course of action.
5. Acts 12:5 and 12:12 show us New Testament believers meeting together for prayer. How can corporate prayer be of benefit? Is it something that you prioritise in your life?

Even Out of Control is in God's Control

👉 *Read ESTHER 5:9 – 6:14*

There's a tragedy in this story of Esther that I've always missed. It's the story of a man so consumed with selfishness that he failed to see the danger of his chosen course. As he ran headlong into conflict with the Almighty God he was oblivious of the consequences of his allegiance with Satan.

Perhaps Haman didn't even believe in the devil, but the devil certainly believed in him – in his loyalty, in his determination to destroy and his hatred of God. The appalling fact is that apart from a brief time of wealth and power, there was absolutely nothing in it for him. Whereas God's children are loved and promised care, a future and reward, Satan doesn't reserve one ounce of affection for his.

Even at the height of his career so far, we see that Satan is destroying Haman (5:9–14). His emotions are wrecked.

No stability

Haman is on an emotional roller coaster, on the day of Esther's first feast he's

- Happy and high-spirited (v. 9).
- Furious (v. 9).
- Restrained (v. 10).
- Hospitable (v. 10).
- Conceited (vv. 11, 12).
- Excited and filled with anticipation (v. 12).
- Despairing and frustrated (v. 13).
- Feels immense pleasure and decisiveness (v. 14).

And the rumour among men is that women are hormonal!

No satisfaction

At the height of his career and excesses, Mick Jagger sang, 'I can't get no satisfaction.' Here's Haman at the peak of his, failing to enjoy his success and the honour shown to him by the Royal Couple. It was a rare privilege to enjoy an intimate dinner with both of them, yet all this is meaningless, simply because one man again refuses to grovel. Haman convinces us of the truth that, 'Just as Death and Destruction are never satisfied, so human desire is never satisfied.' (Prov. 27:20)

No patience

Mordecai's living under the cloud of a death sentence, but Haman can't wait that long. Death by the sword will not do either. There had to be a punishment for Mordecai much more terrifying and humiliating. He wants to make an example of him.

No true friends

We don't know if Haman felt lonely, but he was very much alone because the advice of his friends is fundamentally flawed. They share his ambition and advise him in a way they know he wants to hear. To make matters worse, his wife Zeresh doesn't help him at all. The fact she is mentioned by name twice in verses 9–14 leaves us in no doubt that her role in this is significant. She could have calmed him down and challenged him. But instead, this fiercely ambitious woman eggs him on. She stands with the majority rather than by the side of her husband for his good.

No humility

Pride produced a wrong opinion of himself. It raised him to such a point that he honestly felt that no one compared with him in the king's eyes. From there, the only way was down, and when he fell, his humiliation was great.

Satan traps us into believing that our worth is bound up in how much acclaim we receive and how much we're noticed. With that perspective comes disappointment, discontentment, selfishness, ambition and jealousy.

One year our family holiday was spent in a kindly loaned luxury apartment. Everything was wonderful until the day I got chatting to the couple that owned the penthouse flat upstairs. I discovered the man was a football manager and their main home was in a very exclusive part of London. From that moment on I was *desperate* they wouldn't ask where I lived or what I, or my husband, do for a living. From that point the day was ruined. Feelings of embarrassment and inadequacy filled me. Despite the abundant blessings that are mine I began to feel discontented and became more irritable and angry as the day went on.

James writes, 'For jealousy and selfishness are not God's kind of wisdom. Such things are earthly, unspiritual, and motivated by the Devil. For wherever there is jealousy and selfish ambition, there you will find disorder and every kind of evil.' (Jas 3:15–16)

When our self-worth is based predominantly on how others view us, we will crave to be the centre of attention. How we see ourselves won't be grounded in reality and if unchecked this need for affirmation will become destructive.

Note James' words 'every kind of evil.'

Our friendships may be obsessive and possessive. Our children will be pressurized to always excel so that their success will reflect well on us. If we're single we may feel permanently inadequate, less worthy and somehow less feminine than our married friends. When we as wives don't get the attention we feel we deserve from our husbands we might look elsewhere. Our morals and opinions will shift along with the beliefs of others. We will be too aware of our image and appearance. Becoming older will disproportionately bother us. We will be marked by a lack of contentment.

The danger is that we like Haman can look to others to bring us fulfillment when in truth only God has that power.

Satan – Limited Time, Limited Power

Charles Haddon Spurgeon, the nineteenth-century preacher, preached a number of sermons that were put into book form and entitled *Satan: A Defeated Foe.*

What a compelling title for a book! Although Satan continues to fight against God's glory, Christ overcame his main weapon death, on the cross and through his resurrection.

Spurgeon writes this about Satan:

> . . . he is persuaded that his reign is ended and that his
> opportunity is short. Satan feels about him even now a
> chain, which is lengthened for a while, but which shall be
> drawn up shorter about him and tightened down by-
> and-by. Then he shall roam the earth no longer, but lie as
> a captive in his prison house.[1]

Satan knows that his time is short, yet hates God so
much that he's determined to do all that he can to wreck
God's glory. There seems to be an element of Satan pan-
icking in verses 9 to 14. He perhaps was taken aback by
these responses.

1) God's people on their knees, crying for help and deliverance

The eighteenth-century poet William Cowper recognized the impact of prayer on Satan when he wrote,
'Satan trembles when he sees the weakest saint upon his
knees.'[2]

2) Esther's determination to confront evil

3) Mordecai's continued refusal to bow

Let's remind ourselves of God's promises in Jeremiah
chapter 29.

> ". . . For I know the plans they have for you," says the
> LORD. "They are plans for good and not for disaster, to
> give you a future and a hope. In those days when you
> pray, I will listen. If you look for me in earnest, you will
> find me when you seek me. I will be found by you," says
> the LORD. "I will end your captivity and restore your for-
> tunes. I will gather you out of the nations where I sent
> you and bring you home again to your own land. (vv.
> 11–14)

Satan doesn't need to be reminded of God's promises – he knows them more than we do. So when he sees how God's people respond in faith, he knows his time is short and tries to outwit God by taking him by surprise. Mordecai would be struck down long before the preplanned execution date. Just in case he can't destroy the entire Jewish race, he'd have Mordecai anyway! In fury Satan incites Haman even more. But he oversteps the mark. As the extremely high pole is erected, it seems he will win – yet in the event it's God who is outwitting Satan.

Spurgeon said:

> Oftentimes the development of evil is an indication that there is an equal or a greater development of good, and that the climax of ill is frequently its end. Do you not know that in the world of nature the darkest time of the night is that which precedes the dawning of the day? . . . Even so, when evil is at its height, it is nearest to its fall.[3]

Recently in the middle of a crisis I prayed repeatedly over several days for deliverance. As the situation seemed to worsen I cried, 'Lord, I've been praying and praying, and I've got to be honest, it doesn't seem you are listening.'

I wonder if the Jews prayed like that, as they heard the hammering from Haman's courtyard, and as the rumours spread of Mordecai's planned execution. As they looked up at the 75-foot gallows, did they ask what the point of the last few days of fasting had been? Did God seem further away than ever? The fact that Harbona in 7:9 knew what Haman was planning shows that Haman's plan wasn't a secret.

Yet by that very night we're reminded that God is still very much in control, and by the morning we should be convinced.

That night the king had trouble sleeping, so he ordered an attendant to bring the historical records of his kingdom so they could be read to him. In those records he discovered an account of how Mordecai had exposed the plot of Bigthana and Teresh, two of the eunuchs who guarded the door to the king's private quarters. They had plotted to assassinate the king. '"What reward or recognition did we ever give Mordecai for this?" the king asked. His attendants replied, "Nothing has been done."' (Esth. 6:3)

We see that God controls:

1. History

Did Mordecai ever think back to the time he saved the king's life and wonder what it was all about? Perhaps it was so long ago he rarely thought about it. On the surface, perhaps, as he thanked God for enabling him to keep Esther's position secure, he could have had no idea that his actions actually contributed to keeping a whole nation safe.

The proverb asks, 'How can we understand the road we travel? It is the LORD who directs our steps.' (Prov. 20:24)

This whole truth is so encouraging and exciting. Lots of things in my past seem to have been pointless. It's easy to wonder what I've done with my life up to now. All those people I've spoken to about Christ yet seen no response. Those times I have stood up for what was right yet seen no change in the situation. Why did I bother? Here I'm reminded that I can never know how God can use my faithfulness to him in the past for present and future glory to him. And that changes how I view today as well. It gives today a purpose.

2. No thanks

If there's one thing I hate, it's when I stop to give way to another driver, who then races past without acknowledging me. It really makes me mad! So I dread to think what my reaction would have been if I'd saved the life of the sovereign and received no recognition.

For five years Mordecai had been ignored and unrewarded by the king, whose life he'd saved. How often we give up on things, because no one says 'Thank you'. How often our willing service becomes grudging service, because no one pats us on the back. Don't get me wrong here – thanks and encouragement are important. Paul is full of praise in his letters, even to the churches who need challenging (such as the church in Corinth).

Yet whereas Haman was completely thrown by what he saw as a lack of recognition from the king, Mordecai shows us that a lack of recognition shouldn't deter us from continuing to do the right thing.

Five years later, and he's just as faithful to his God. Why? Because while Haman was encouraged by what men thought of him, Mordecai realized he was answerable to God. It was what God thought of him that mattered. And God's reward is always immeasurably more wonderful than other people's acclaim.

Even the fact that he wasn't thanked up to now by Xerxes was completely in God's control. The lack of acclaim at the time it should have been given, made it all the more effective when it came. God had not forgotten. If he'd been thanked at the time, God couldn't have used this now, for his purpose. So even when we live and work among the most ungrateful of people we should remember that God knows and controls even that.

3. The king

'The king's heart is like a stream of water, directed by the LORD; he turns it wherever he pleases.' (Prov. 21:1)

God controlled Xerxes' sleep patterns, thoughts, and even his reading material. He pricked his conscience and planted the desire in him to reward Mordecai.

The passage indicates that Xerxes couldn't sleep because something was troubling him. He didn't know what it was, but something told him it might be to do with the past few years – something he'd done or something he'd missed. So he called for the court diaries.

Even the greatest man on earth was not beyond God's control then and neither is he today. It's probably easier to look back on a dead king and believe that of him. It's harder though to believe it of the great and powerful today. Wouldn't you have thought that a king with insomnia would have called for one of his women from the harem or one of his musicians to play a soothing melody? Couldn't he have wandered the palace, delighting in his treasures or asked for something to eat? No! Not when God had hold of his heart.

4. Haman the enemy of the Jews

'Who is that in the outer court?' the king inquired. Now, as it happened, Haman had just arrived in the outer court of the palace to ask the king to hang Mordecai from the gallows he'd prepared.

Proverbs 19:21 reminds us that, 'You can make many plans, but the LORD's purpose will prevail.'

All Haman's plans for evil were being turned on their head. God controlled the timing of his arrival to perfection. Even his super-inflated ego was in God's hands. It meant that Mordecai's reward was even more spectacular and his own humiliation greater than it would otherwise have been.

In actual fact, the king still appreciated him hugely. He'd loved Haman's suggestion of reward. 'Excellent!' was his response. Not only that, but he gave Haman the honour of carrying out this important task. Haman had suggested that, 'one of the king's most noble princes . . . dress the man in the king's robe and lead him . . . on the king's own horse.' Xerxes thought Haman the ideal choice to play the part of noble prince. But yet again, Haman found it impossible to appreciate his position. Unless he was top dog, all other honour was pointless. He worshipped himself and wanted everyone else to worship him too.

But he was reminded that he was not God. Who by? By the very same wife and friends who only hours before had basked in the glory of his power. God controlled them too. When the time was right he revealed the truth of the matter to them.

> When Haman told his wife, Zeresh, and all his friends what had happened, they said, "Since Mordecai—this man who has humiliated you—is a Jew, you will never succeed in your plans against him. It will be fatal to continue to oppose him." While they were still talking, the king's eunuchs arrived to take Haman to the banquet Esther had prepared. (Esth. 6:13,14)

They suddenly recognized there was someone more powerful than Haman fighting for Mordecai. Unfortunately for Haman it came too late for him to change his course.

Haman was never completely out of control. Even in the control of Satan, he was ultimately in God's.

There's something about this selfish ambition that is visible in Haman, which makes me shudder. He was an evil and godless man. He hated God. But it's not what I see in him that scares me, it's what he shows me of myself. The truth is that even in me, a child of God and one who genuinely loves my Father, I see traces of that same sinful drive.

James, the apostle recognized it in the church and wrote to the Jewish Christians scattered among the nations:

> What is causing the quarrels and fights among you? Isn't it the whole army of evil desires at war within you? You want what you don't have, so you scheme and kill to get it. You are jealous for what others have, and you can't possess it, so you fight and quarrel to take it away from them. And yet the reason you don't have what you want is that you don't ask God for it. And even when you do ask, you don't get it because your whole motive is wrong—you want only what will give you pleasure. (Jas. 4:1–3)

It's that desire, even in the church and my family to have things *my* way. It's that craving for recognition and praise or that jealousy for other women's possessions, gifts, position or roles. I can be an expert in kidding myself it's not there and can justify myself by criticizing others and excusing myself. But the evidence is there in the conflict I often cause.

Rather than my life, thoughts and words revolving around God, they revolve around me. Rather than worshipping him, I worship me. Rather than recognizing what he's given me, I concentrate on what he hasn't given me. I fight against his will for my life because I know better. The result? I lack joy and contentment and take it out on everyone else around me.

And it's not just me is it? That's why we have disputes and rifts in our churches. They're not usually over the fundamentals of our faith, but more often about style and preference. James continues in verse 4 'You adulterers! Don't you realize that friendship with this world makes you an enemy of God?'

But I'm not a lost unbeliever like Haman was. What can I do about it? How can I get back to the recognition of who my controller is?

The answer comes through the rest of James chapter 4. He tells us to do what Haman didn't do.

> So humble yourselves before God. Resist the Devil, and he will flee from you. Draw close to God, and God will draw close to you. Wash your hands, you sinners; purify your hearts, you hypocrites. Let there be tears for the wrong things you have done. Let there be sadness instead of laughter, and gloom instead of joy. When you bow down before the Lord and admit your dependence on him, he will lift you up and give you honor. (vv. 7–10)

Very simply, James gives us a five-step plan.

1. *Respect* who God is, as the controller of all things.
2. *Remember* he desires good for me, not bad.
3. *Repent* of putting my desires in the place of God.
4. *Refuse* to believe Satan's lies that God is some kind of celestial killjoy.
5. *Result*? I am free to control my ambitions, rather than my ambition controlling me, and I receive honour that matters, straight from the eternal God.

5. Mordecai's steps

I'd love to know what was going through Mordecai's mind as he rode on the back of that horse, looking down at the back of his enemy's head. What a bizarre experience it must have been. Perhaps he knew of what Haman had in mind for him and could even see the pole standing high in the distance. Did he sense this was a foretaste of the genuine power and acclaim that was about to come to him within hours? He must have had an assurance of the truth that 'The steps of a good man are ordered by the Lord.'

For us Mordecai's a living example of James' assurance: 'When you bow down before the Lord and admit your dependence on him, he will lift you up and give you honor.' (Jas. 4:10)

This could only be of God. And Mordecai recognized that for when it was all over he quietly returned to his position in the king's staff to see what would happen next.

There was no gathering together of his friends and family for a bragging party. In this time of honour, he retained his humility, faithfully getting on with what God had called him to do. In this he gave the glory to the God who controls all things.

Because Mordecai responded to success as well as persecution in a godly and submissive way, he shows himself ready for the greater challenge ahead.

Questions for Personal Reflection

1. Often as women we can feel as if we're on an emotional roller coaster. Hormones can play a big part in this, but what other factors can affect us?

2. How do jealousy and selfish ambition manifest themselves in your life? What effect does this have on those around you?

3. What should our response be when Satan fools us into believing that he's in control? How can we remind ourselves of God's sovereignty?

8

Courage to Confront

☞ *Read ESTHER 7*

Chapter 7 of the Book of Esther has got to be one of the most dramatic scenes in the Bible. The focus is on one table around which three people sit. Yet as they share the same meal and make polite conversation, their feelings couldn't have been more different. Haman's forced laughter and fake smile covered turbulent emotions. We can be sure he wasn't enjoying this feast as much as the previous day.

He'd spent the day publicly acclaiming his arch-enemy, tramping around the city square and shouting until he was hoarse. He'd rushed home to lick his wounds, but with barely time to get everything off his chest, was collected for Esther's banquet. He was unprepared, flustered, and as he was rushed away the words ringing in his ears were, 'Since Mordecai – this man who has humiliated you – is a Jew, you will never succeed in your plans against him.' (6:13)

Yet as he brooded, he was unafraid. He still had no idea of Esther's nationality or relationship to Mordecai. He had no premonition as he feasted that the gallows he has erected for another are actually ready and waiting for him.

Queen Esther across the table knew what lay ahead yet remained composed, dignified and clear-headed. There's every chance she was aware of the pole erected for her uncle. Harbona, one of the king's eunuchs who was present knew (v. 9). Yet she remained the perfect hostess.

And then there was Xerxes, enjoying excellent food and wine in the company of his best friend, and his beautiful, intriguing wife. So again, he asks, 'Tell me what you want, Queen Esther. What is your request? I will give it to you, even if it is half the kingdom.' (v. 2)

This is the opportunity she's been waiting for. There's no delay, 'And so Queen Esther replied'. And what a reply it is as she pleads for her life and the lives of her people.

> "Who would do such a thing?" King Xerxes demanded. "Who would dare touch you?"
>
> Esther replied, "This wicked Haman is our enemy." Haman grew pale with fright before the king and queen. Then the king jumped to his feet in a rage and went out into the palace garden.
>
> But Haman stayed behind to plead for his life with Queen Esther, for he knew that he was doomed. In despair he fell on the couch where Queen Esther was reclining, just as the king was returning from the palace garden. "Will he even assault the queen right here in the palace, before my very eyes?" the king roared. And as soon as the king spoke, his attendants covered Haman's face, signaling his doom. (Esth. 7:5–8)

Just the night before Xerxes had been remembering an assassination attempt. Just that day he had rewarded a loyal man. For the last hour or so he'd felt relaxed and safe in a warm environment with those he trusted. Now, he was reminded that he was under constant threat even from those he considered his friends (approximately eight years later, King Xerxes was actually assassinated). Perhaps he believed that Haman's wish was to destroy him as well, as his queen. When he returned from the garden and found Haman on Esther's couch pleading for his life, he believed the worst.

Haman's end comes swiftly. He dies, alone yet seen by all. I wonder if the Jews looked up at his body swinging high above them, and remembered Isaiah's words. 'He judges the great people of the world and brings them all to nothing. They hardly get started, barely taking root, when he blows on them and their work withers. The wind carries them off like straw.' (Is. 40:23)

I hate confrontation. I might do it but I don't enjoy it and there are many times when I avoid it at all costs. Most of this is linked with fear.

- Fear of dealing with the situation in a way that will make things worse.
- Fear of what others will think of me.
- Fear of what they will say of me.
- Fear of their reaction and counter accusations.
- Fear of my temper (which I find more difficult to control when I'm nervous).
- Fear of the possible consequences.

In all, the lazy side of me begs me to ignore things and keep quiet. Perhaps you don't have any problems with speaking your mind, but maybe *the way* you speak is the problem.

Clementine Churchill wrote a letter of confrontation to her husband Winston at a time of high stress. I wish I could always tackle things with such wisdom:

I hope you will forgive me if I tell you something I feel you ought to know.

One of the men in your entourage (a devoted friend) has been to me & told me that there is a danger of your being generally disliked by your colleagues and subordinates because of your rough sarcastic & overbearing manner . . . I was astonished & upset because in all these years I have been accustomed to all those who have worked with & under you, loving you – I said this, & I was told 'No doubt it's the strain.'

. . .

My Darling Winston. I must confess that I have noticed a deterioration in your manner; & you are not as kind as you used to be . . . with this terrific power you must combine urbanity, kindness and if possible Olympic calm . . . you won't get the best results by irascibility & rudeness . . . Please forgive your loving devoted and watchful

Clemmie.[1]

If you'd been Esther, how would you have handled the situation? Would you have confronted this evil? I like to think I would have been just like her. In reality though, I have to question whether or not I confront sin in the places and situations I'm in now.

In chapter 5, we looked at the inner beauty of a gentle, quiet and submissive spirit. Does this inner beauty rule out the right to confront? Are we never to confront our husbands in our marriages?

Esther shows us that however difficult our husbands are, confrontation is well within the mandate of being helper to them. Yet she also demonstrates there are ways we should do it. And the principles don't just apply to marriage. They apply to how we speak to our parents, friends, children, bosses, teachers, church leaders and everyone else who is making sinful choices or is unaware of things that are going on around them.

Before we look at how Esther tackled the situation, let's look at a couple of examples of other women who, like Esther, were also married to powerful but difficult men.

Jezebel – a domineering and frustrated woman

Jezebel was another queen, married to King Ahab of Israel. We read a vivid account of her in 1 Kings 21:1–16. King Ahab longed for a vineyard that belonged to a God-fearing man called Naboth. Naboth refused to sell or trade, because God had forbidden it.

> So Ahab went home angry and sullen because of Naboth's answer. The king went to bed with his face to the wall and refused to eat!
>
> "What in the world is the matter?" his wife, Jezebel, asked him. "What has made you so upset that you are not eating?"
>
> "I asked Naboth to sell me his vineyard or trade it, and he refused!" Ahab told her.
>
> "Are you the king of Israel or not?" Jezebel demanded. "Get up and eat and don't worry about it. I'll get you Naboth's vineyard!"
>
> So she wrote letters in Ahab's name, sealed them with his seal, and sent them to the elders and other leaders of the city where Naboth lived. In her letters she commanded: "Call the citizens together for fasting and prayer, and give Naboth a place of honor. Find two scoundrels who will accuse him of cursing God and the king. Then take him out and stone him to death."
>
> So the elders and other leaders followed the instructions Jezebel had written in the letters. They called for a

fast and put Naboth at a prominent place before the people. Then two scoundrels accused him before all the people of cursing God and the king. So he was dragged outside the city and stoned to death. The city officials then sent word to Jezebel, "Naboth has been stoned to death."

When Jezebel heard the news, she said to Ahab, "You know the vineyard Naboth wouldn't sell you? Well, you can have it now! He's dead!" So Ahab immediately went down to the vineyard to claim it. (1 Kgs. 21:4–16)

This passage tells us quite a bit about Ahab. What a baby! He was sulky, selfish, greedy and discontented. He didn't care a jot for God's laws, or his people, but despite that, was too spineless to get what he wanted.

There's a sin issue here, but Jezebel doesn't see it as a problem. Her motives are skewed because she worships Baal and herself rather than God. She's not bothered about God's glory, but she's bothered about hers. So how does she react?

1. With frustration. It's not the vineyard that's a problem for her. She's dissatisfied with her husband. He's not the leader she thinks he should be so she confronts him by asking him the equivalent of 'Are you a man or a mouse?' Her power and image is at stake.
2. She took the lead. She shows herself to be the boss in their marriage, and in the land. Without discussion, she did what she thought best.
3. She used fear as her weapon. The seal gave the letters the royal mandate, implying there would be punishment for those who disobeyed. She called for fasting and prayer, but this was a cover of false spirituality. It was a means to an evil end. It implied to

the people that they needed to repent before God would avert judgment. Naboth was revealed as the culprit. In reality Jezebel was an idolatress (1 Kgs.16:31–32).

4. She used lies to get what she wanted. She wrote in Ahab's name, and the whole plot was based on fabrication.
5. She promoted injustice. Jezebel was heartless and showed no compassion for the godly Naboth.
6. She twisted God's laws to suit her own ends.

- She used blasphemy laws, which was punishable by death.
- The Mosaic Law required two witnesses in capital cases (Num. 35:30; Deut. 17:6; 19:5).
- Naboth was killed in a place that was in accordance with the Mosaic Law (Lev. 24:14; Num.15:35–36).

7. She used others to cover her tracks. Scoundrels literally means 'Son of Belial' or Satan. This was a Hebrew way of saying base, wicked or worthless men.
8. She influenced her husband but for evil not good.

No one else so completely sold himself to what was evil in the LORD's sight as did Ahab, for his wife, Jezebel, influenced him. He was especially guilty because he worshiped idols just as the Amorites had done—the people whom the Lord had driven from the land ahead of the Israelites. (21:25–26)

9. Both of them were held accountable for their idolatry and their treatment of Naboth. God sent the prophet Elijah to Ahab with judgment.

I have come because you have sold yourself to what is evil in the Lord's sight. The Lord is going to bring disaster to you and sweep you away. He will not let a single one of your male descendants, slave or free alike, survive in Israel! He is going to destroy your family as he did the family of Jeroboam son of Nebat and the family of Baasha son of Ahijah, for you have made him very angry and have led all of Israel into sin. The LORD has also told me that the Dogs of Jezreel will eat the body of your wife, Jezebel, at the city wall. The members of your family who die in the city will be eaten by dogs, and those who die in the field will be eaten by vultures. (21:20b–24)

Jezebel was confrontational, but not about sin. Because her motives were wrong, her reactions were wrong.

Zeresh – a selfishly subservient woman

Zeresh lived in the same locality as Esther. Married to the Prime Minister, she was the other influential woman in the kingdom. Haman as we know was ambitious, self-centred, and cruel. There was a great deal of sin in Haman that needed challenging. He was on a sure road to destruction, but this woman ignored all his faults, telling him all he wanted to hear.

1. She never confronted him and in effect she promoted his lies, injustice and cruelty.
2. She flattered him by listening to his bragging, wanting him to be happy, but not wanting what was best.
3. She positively encouraged him in his sinful behaviour, suggesting what he could do to Mordecai.
4. She used people power. She hid behind their friends. She took the crowd's view, even when it came to advising her husband. She was a coward, and not

prepared to stand alone. When their opinion changed, so did hers.

5. She thought only of the short-term benefits to Haman's actions rather than considering the future.
6. She was lawless. God's word never came into the equation.
7. She was held accountable. The fact she's named three times in such a male-dominated society indicates her responsibility before God.
8. She was judged. She lost her husband, her ten sons, her land and property, her friends and her influence.

Zeresh was a weak selfish woman who appears to have wanted a comfortable life at any cost.

Both Jezebel and Zeresh's responses to sin were flawed. Neither were godly reactions, but perhaps if we are honest, we can all remember times when we've seen elements of them in us.

Esther – a strongly submissive woman

Esther's husband had already deposed one queen. His temper was legendary. He's protected under layer upon layer of etiquette, and yet remains vulnerable. His image is glorious, and yet he's discontented. The main issue, which Esther needs to confront, is that he's let his guard down to a man of great evil, who he's trusted too much to question. He hasn't explored the issues behind the proposed atrocity, and will have the blood of a nation on his hands.

> And so Queen Esther replied, "If Your Majesty is pleased with me and wants to grant my request, my petition is that my life, and the lives of my people will be spared.

For my people and I have been sold to those who would kill, slaughter, and annihilate us. If we had only been sold as slaves, I could remain quiet, for that would have been a matter too trivial to warrant disturbing the king." (Esth. 7:3–6)

What can we learn from Esther?

1. She planned. Prayer and fasting weren't a smoke-screen of false spirituality, but a means of preparation. Esther knew this was the key to unlock God's blessing and guidance. It prepared her heart and attitude and was the means of preparing the king's too.
2. She chose her the moment carefully. She blessed her husband. She created a warm atmosphere rather than a strained one.
3. She used God's power not her own. Esther didn't manipulate Xerxes, using either sex or tears.
4. She spoke the truth. She was honest about who she was and explained what she knew. She didn't exaggerate or downplay the situation.
5. She was clear in her speech.
6. She was gracious and respectful.
7. She spoke with passion for God's glory and compassion for God's people.
8. She was courageous. She didn't hide behind other people, getting them to confront her husband for her. She singled herself out as one who was under a death sentence. She aligned herself with her people.
9. She promoted justice, and God's law.
10. She emphasised the seriousness of the matter. 'If we had only been sold as slaves, I could remain quiet, for that would have been a matter too trivial to warrant disturbing the king.' (v. 4)

11. She took the initiative, but not the lead. She didn't lecture Xerxes how to sort this out, but left the ball in his court.

12. She handled the situation with wisdom and patience. She didn't blurt out an accusation of Haman straight away, but waits, putting Proverbs 16:21 into practice, 'The wise are known for their understanding, and instruction is appreciated if it's well presented.' She believed that 'Patience can persuade a prince, and soft speech can crush strong opposition' (Prov. 25:15)

13. She makes herself vulnerable, showing her powerlessness.

14. Her words are free of bitterness, resentment or frustration.

The success of her godly approach was outstanding. Her method of confrontation was perfectly matched to how she'd lived above reproach as queen, the result being that she was taken seriously. She was believed 100 per cent – not just by her husband but by Haman, who immediately 'grew pale with fright before the king and queen' (v. 6). The king was so convinced of the truth that Haman knew that only Esther held the key to his escape.

Esther influenced her husband for good. Not only for the good of herself, her people and her God, but also for *his* good. He as well as Haman would have been held accountable for the annihilation of the Jews.

Someone called King Lemuel in Proverbs 31:10–12 asks 'Who can find a virtuous and capable wife? She is worth more than precious rubies. Her husband can trust her, and she will greatly enrich his life. She will not hinder him, but help him all her life.'

That's not to say that every time we confront sin, God will give us the success we desire. It may result in the loss of a marriage, a relationship or even a job.

In some cases, we might need to take our issues to another level such as church leadership, senior management or even a court of law.

At times, the situation might worsen so much that we can't do anything else except find comfort and refuge in God, with the realization we are suffering for righteousness sake and that he is our judge.

> This suffering is all part of what God has called you too. Christ who suffered for you, is your example. Follow in his steps. He never sinned, and he never deceived anyone. He did not retaliate when he was insulted. When he suffered, he did not threaten or get even. He left his case in the hands of God, who always judges fairly. (1 Pet. 2:21–23)

A friend recounted a conversation she had with her rebellious teenage daughter. Her daughter told her to 'Get off her back.' Her mum replied, 'No. I will *not* get off your back. God has entrusted you to me and I am accountable to him how I bring you up.'

That is why we bother to confront others. Our style may change slightly depending on the person we're confronting, but Esther's godly principles remain.

A short corridor of calm

> On that same day King Xerxes gave the estate of Haman, the enemy of the Jews, to Queen Esther. Then Mordecai was brought before the king, for Esther had told the king how they were related. The King took off his signet ring—which he had taken back from Haman—and gave it to Mordecai. And Esther

appointed Mordecai to be in charge of Haman's property. (8:1–2)

For a short time, there's an initial ease in tension. The king's anger has abated. Esther explains her relationship to Mordecai, and everything is out in the open at last. Xerxes is sorry for all that's happened and tries to make it up to them. In his usual style he lavishes generous gifts on them – the very gifts he'd given to Haman, so demonstrating his change of allegiance.

I love the bit about the signet ring, 'which he had taken back from Haman—and given to Mordecai. (I wonder if Haman knew as this symbol of authority was snatched away, whose finger it would be on within hours!)

Then, it's as if there's a pause while Esther and Mordecai wait for the king to bring up the delicate subject of the annihilation of the Jews. When nothing is forthcoming, it seems to dawn on Esther that the immensity of the problem hasn't quite sunk in. The main issue remains the same.

The courage to confront again

> Now once more Esther came before the king, falling down at his feet and begging him with tears to stop Haman's evil plot against the Jews. Again the king held out the gold scepter to Esther. So she rose and stood before him and said, "If your Majesty is pleased with me and if he thinks it is right, send out a decree reversing Haman's orders to destroy the Jews throughout all the provinces of the king. For how can I endure to see my people and my family slaughtered and destroyed?" (8:3–6)

Xerxes' anger has been pacified, but he's failed to pacify Esther. So she confronts him again. She sees the door open into his heart, and sensing that it might not be open for long, she enters. I believe this shows the greatest courage of all so far. Why? Because now she has even more to lose. Let's look at the dangers she faces this time.

- She risks a better or improved marriage. After a month of estrangement her husband has welcomed her, enjoyed her company, listened to her, protected her and honoured both her and her cousin Mordecai. He has even killed his friend for her. Wouldn't it be easier to keep the peace?
- She risks losing both her own and Mordecai's recent and substantial honour and property. Life is getting good.
- She risks seeming ungrateful. Xerxes has shown kindness, and this second confrontation might appear that she was throwing his gifts back in his face. He's answered the first part of her request after all.

As a minister's wife, I admit it's hard to confront people about their sin when they've been generous to us as a family in the past.

Politicians are required to declare the gifts they receive from wealthy friends and contacts. If they don't, and they're found out there's a scandal because we're suspicious of the donor having undue influence on the government. We recognize rightly that it's harder to stand up for what we believe to be right when we're laden down with gifts.

- Esther ran the risk of being accused of nagging! Proverbs tells us that, 'a nagging wife annoys like a constant dripping.' (19:13b)

  The Oxford Dictionary defines nagging as annoying or irritating (a person) with persistent complaining, criticizing, or urging.2 We can't accuse Esther of this when we look at her words but a temperamental husband could.

To my shame when my husband reminds me of something I haven't done (but should have) my harsh retort sometimes is, 'Oh stop nagging me!' I haven't got the power of the king but even my reaction can be scary.

We often don't mention things more than once because we don't want to be accused of nagging. This didn't put Esther off though. She recognized there's a time to shut up, but also a time to speak, and that this might be her last opportunity.

- There was a danger posed by her tears. We've already looked at the etiquette surrounding the king. No one was even allowed to appear sad before him as it suggested he was not a capable ruler. Yet Esther fell at his feet, weeping. What could that have said to Xerxes about how she feels about his rule and handling of the situation?

There are people who can't cope with any sign of vulnerability or weakness. Years ago, I was in terrible conflict with another woman and eventually went to sort things out. After getting nowhere, I felt so desperate I cried. I was stunned when she shouted at me impatiently to get a grip on myself! Perhaps she was used to people who manipulated through tears and we have to be careful not to do that to get what we want. But showing true vulnerability is always a risky business – especially in conflict. It immediately opens us up for counter-attack or misunderstanding. Tears will often make the other person feel guilty and the response can be anger.

Esther wasn't interested in temporal happiness and ease. Luxury, honour and a better marriage weren't enough. She still wanted more, *much* more. She wanted the lives of her people. And so, she bares her soul before the king when she knows he's listening. Again, she speaks with the same respect as before, 'If Your Majesty is pleased with me and if he thinks it is right.'

She then suggests what he could do without telling him what he must do. She recognizes that this is up to him now. Her responsibility might soon be over, but she reminds him of his power to change the situation. She's still humble, still passionate, and still respectful. 'For how can I endure to see my people, and my family slaughtered and destroyed?' As she bares her soul, she asks the question how will she cope, if this isn't resolved? Perhaps the starkness of this question, combined with her urgency, perseverance and courage propelled him to make the speech in verses 7 and 8.

Xerxes suggests that all along his motive for hanging Haman had been because of his plans to destroy the Jews. We can't measure whether this was his intent or not, and it probably doesn't matter anyway. What matters to us is that yet again Esther was faithful again in the face of personal loss.

Is this kind of confrontation idealistic? Yes.

Is it possible? Yes.

Is it difficult? Yes.

Will it take discipline? Yes – loads of it.

Esther was extra careful in the way she spoke because the stakes were so high. If I considered the results of every time I speak wouldn't I be more controlled and careful?

Do you confront Esther's way?

Questions for Personal Reflection

Are there any issues that you need to be confronting with another person? Use the questions below to examine your motives and approach.

Confrontation checklist

1. Are you ignoring behaviour that should be challenged for an easy and quiet life? Does it seem easier to flatter? Do you find you get on further in life by telling people what they want to hear?
2. Are you challenging behaviour that's contrary to God's law, or is it based purely on your opinion or preferences? Whose glory and good are you promoting? Yours or God's?
3. Are you concerned with the person's spiritual good or are you frustrated or bitter with them?
4. Do truth, justice and compassion motivate you, or do you use fear as a weapon? Are others afraid of your temper, cruelty and sulkiness if they don't respond as you want?
5. Have you prayed seriously for wisdom in dealing with the situation? Have you prayerfully planned your words, seeking advice when appropriate?
6. Is your own conscience clear, remembering you will be accountable for your words and actions before God?
7. Do you recognize that ultimately it's God who changes another's heart, not you?
8. Are you prepared to respond with humility if things don't turn out in the way you desire?

9

Blessings and Weapons of War

☞ *Read ESTHER 8:1–9:19*

'On that day, the enemies of the Jews had hoped to destroy them, but quite the opposite happened.' (9:1b)

If there's a statement that sums up the Book of Esther, it has to be that one. It's the story in a nutshell.

A declaration of God's deliverance.

A reminder of his faithfulness.

A demonstration of his power.

How many times in history have the enemies of God's people hoped to destroy them, only to find they have become stronger than ever? It would be impossible to count. That's what persecution often does. Ultimately it can strengthen and grow those who are his.

Charles Spurgeon wrote, 'Satan is a lackey to the Almighty.'[1] What he means is that however much he rebels, and fights against God and his people, ultimately that is all Satan is – an unwilling servant.

God wanted to give the Jews much more than they had already, and it was Satan, who delivered it to them on a plate, even through persecution. We might not understand God's reasoning but we, like Augustine, have to trust him. He stated 'God judged it better to bring good out of evil than to suffer no evil to exist.'[2]

God gave them all the weapons they needed, and these weapons are also blessings. In Esther 8:9–17 we read about four weapons that God gave to his people.

1. Strong leadership.
2. Worship and celebration.
3. Unity and community.
4. Purity.

And these all secured growth.

Weapon number 1 – strong leadership

After reading Esther 8:7–14 don't you feel like we've been here before? The king's secretaries are summoned. They take dictation, which they translate into numerous languages. They structure their notes into edicts concerning the identical enforcement date, which are authorized by the Royal name and stamp of Xerxes. The first-class courier service is again employed to deliver the mail throughout the entire empire.

Yet this time the Jews are at the top of the mailing list. This letter isn't just about them, but for them. Rather than death and despair comes life and hope. It doesn't promise an easy ride, but it does grant them the authority to fight.

Why the change in fortune? God has performed a revolution in the leadership of the land. Mordecai and Esther are in charge. What a weapon! What a blessing!

I'm familiar with the demands of leadership. Over the years I've had various leadership responsibilities. As a wife it's my privilege, despite the occasional pain, to help and support my husband not only as the leader of our home, but also over the last eleven or so years as a church minister. It's my considered opinion that it's tough being a good leader. Notice I use the word 'good'. It's not leading necessarily that's so hard but leading well.

What characteristics are we to value and pray for in our leadership – whether in ourselves or in others? Let's look at Mordecai (and later Esther) to help us.

Mordecai:

- Remained awake. Mordecai recognized danger. Even though Haman is dead, lives are at stake, and so is God's glory. He's not blinded by his personal honour and position to the situation that still exists for his people.
- Was able to relay responsibility. If it's not easy being a good leader, it's not particularly easy being a good follower either is it? Perhaps like me you find it simpler to find fault and play the blame game with those in authority. But just because we might not carry the whole weight of overall responsibility on our backs like our leaders do, there's no let-out clause for followers.

  Remember what the greatest leader who ever lived said to his disciples? 'If any of you wants to be my follower, you must put aside your selfish ambition, shoulder your cross, and follow me.' (Mt. 16:24) What does the leader Mordecai call his followers to do? Fight! His message is urgent. This isn't going to be sorted out without them taking up arms. Mordecai not only issued hope, but a battle cry.

- Promoted peace not panic. He was urgent, but not rushed, which allowed him the time to plan strategically. It was over two months since Haman's death warrant for the Jews had been sent out. So it appears that Mordecai took a little time discussing the best course of action. There is confidence in the new edict that God is in control, and no doubt at all they will be delivered.

- Was clear not complicated. His message was straightforward, rather than confusing. Everyone would have understood it. Mordecai used the best tools and services at his disposal. He didn't half-heartedly spread the news like a game of Chinese whispers. What was good enough for Haman was good enough for him. Nothing was left to chance, every eventuality was considered.

- Rather than being idolized, he identified himself with his people. Mordecai's motives were sensitive and unselfish. They were God-driven for the good of others.

'Then Mordecai put on the royal robe of blue and white and the great crown of gold, and he wore an outer cloak of fine linen and purple.' (8:15) He didn't gloat and parade his power, while his people still shook under their death sentence. It wasn't until Mordecai had sorted everything out for others privately, he allowed himself to celebrate by dressing in his royal robes publicly. Don't you love that thought? He only assumed his position in the foreground, after all the hard work was done in the background. He is a leader who does the best for the people even when the world is not watching.

Do you remember what Haman did after his decree was issued? 'Then the king and Haman sat down to drink, but the city of Susa fell into confusion.' (3:15b) But there had been no ivory-tower dining for Mordecai away from the pain of his people. By the time Mordecai publicly associates himself with both King and God, he and his community could rejoice together.

> And the people of Susa celebrated the new decree. The Jews
> were filled with joy and gladness and were honored every-
> where. In every city and province, wherever the king's
> decree arrived, the Jews rejoiced and had a great celebration
> and declared a public festival and holiday. (8:15b–16)

He has shared in their suffering, and now he shares in
their joy.

- Was God-empowered (9:3–4). All Mordecai's success
  was due to God's providence and continued blessing.
  God put him there and kept him there for a reason.
  How else could this humble Jew land this position
  without any wheeling or dealing?

  When we come to look at his attitude in the next
  chapter, we can be assured by his continued humility
  and faithfulness that Mordecai recognized who his
  controller was.
- Showed strength in sharing the vision. In Esther
  9:5–14 we see how Mordecai's leadership was
  strengthened because of his united vision with Esther.
  She didn't step back and let Mordecai get on with it.
  She was right up there with him.

It fascinates me that a man like Xerxes wanted to chat his
situation over with his wife, and not his Prime Minister.
(9:12) Perhaps this desire to protect Esther and to listen
to her indicates a strengthened and improved marriage.
It definitely points to a deepened respect for her opinion
and wishes. Mordecai's position of strength is enhanced
rather than undermined because Esther sees things as he
does. When she has a God-given opportunity to drive
things on, she takes it.

Perhaps Mordecai is otherwise engaged on the front
line or in the control room or he doesn't want to overstep

the mark requesting more of the king. Maybe Esther even sees something that he's missed.

Esther kept herself well informed. She might have been safe in the palace, but Esther didn't distance herself from what was going on outside and with that knowledge she was wise, perceptive and courageous.

The king seems surprised and encouraged at the Jewish success but Esther wasn't squeamish about battling on. She saw the big picture.

She didn't say, 'That's enough fighting!' No way! She was realistic about the continued danger and the consequences of abandoning the fight so soon. She recognized the hotbed of anti-Semitism in the capital. She wanted Haman's already dead sons to be made a spectacle of. She ignored the risk of being labelled an extremist. These enemies needed rooting out. She fought on for love. Love for God's name and love for God's people.

Weapon number 2 – celebration

Did you notice the exuberance packed into Esther 8:15–17?

'Celebrated'

'Filled with joy and gladness'

'Rejoiced and had a great celebration'

'Declared a public festival and holiday'

The kingdom was alive with the sound of songs of deliverance. Not only were they honoured everywhere, but their numbers grew. Those people did not want to be mistaken as their enemies. 'And many of the people of the land became Jews themselves, for they feared what the Jews might do to them.' (Esth. 8:17b)

The Jews didn't go around scowling and cracking their knuckles in anticipation of a showdown. Nor did they quietly retreat into their shells nervously looking ahead and half-heartedly relieved they'd escaped one brush with death.

They knew there was a fight ahead, but they'd been delivered, and they were overflowing with delight. It was a joyful nation, not a miserable one that attracted many non-Jews. And it seems they were warmly embraced.

Today there's not a lot of joy around. Neither the religious nor the irreligious seem to smile much. Stereotypically, the religious angrily try to force their values on others and the irreligious furiously defend their rights for freedom.

It's grace that makes a difference . . . or it should. Haven't we experienced the greatest deliverance ever from sin, Satan's grip and death itself?

Yet as Chuck Swindoll writes:

> Some Christians look like they've been baptized in lemon juice . . . I find it amazing that the only ones on this planet who have every right to smile at the future and enjoy life seldom do. Why, you'd think we have been hired to carry the weight of the world on our shoulders![3]

Do you remember the day you realized you were delivered?

I'd been haunted night after night by the despair that nothing I could do would be good enough for God. As he convicted me of my sin, I grew ever more terrified of death. But the night I realized that Christ had died for me, in my place, and delivered me from sin and from hell itself – how I rejoiced. The joy of deliverance filled my heart until I felt I was floating!

Life is hard. Life is serious. In Ephesians 6:12 Paul tells us, 'We are not fighting against people made of flesh and blood, but against the evil rulers and authorities of the unseen world, against those mighty powers of darkness who rule this world, and against wicked spirits in the heavenly realms.' Yet again and again Paul tells us to rejoice in the Lord our deliverer.

In Philippians 4: 4 he commands, 'Always be full of joy in the Lord. I say it again – rejoice!'

Rejoicing is the natural response to deliverance and aids us in the fight. Several years after these events, Nehemiah reminds the Jews who have returned to Jerusalem for the rebuild of the city walls, '. . . the joy of the Lord is your strength.'

When they remembered what God had already done for them they would be assured of the victory ahead. They would work in the confidence that joy brings. What a weapon! What a blessing!

It was Martin Luther who said, 'Let us sing psalms and spite the devil.'[4] Satan can't cope with hearing God praised and runs with his hands pressed against his ears. Rejoicing produces courage, hope and faith. Without it we become despondent, and defeated.

Bob hated Christianity. For thirty years he'd refused to speak to his brother for becoming a Christian. Yet, over several months, Bob became more and more fascinated as he watched people going in and out of the church near his home. One bright Saturday morning, collecting his newspaper from the local shop he passed a woman cheerfully cleaning the windows of the church porch.

He stopped and said, 'I've been watching the people from your church and I have to ask you, why are you all so happy?' Carol explained it was because Jesus had died to forgive them of their sins.

Bob started attending church and a *Christianity Explored* course. After only weeks of searching, he explained, 'I was driving my car and an Elvis song came on the radio. Joy filled my heart as I sang at the top of my voice, "The wonder of you!" I don't know any Christian songs or hymns, but those words particularly expressed my joy as I suddenly realized what Jesus had done for me on the cross to deliver me from all my sin.'

Only months later, Bob was diagnosed with terminal cancer. Would he have sung deliverance songs if the Christians he saw looked miserable? Would he have faced death with hope and joy if the Christians he watched wore sour expressions? It's a question worth pondering, isn't it?

Yesterday a new Christian explained to our *Christianity Explored* group about her experience of church. She'd attended another church throughout her teens. After thirty years of non-attendance she started coming to ours. 'I can't describe the difference!' She exclaimed. 'I can't wait to get there on a Sunday morning. It's such . . .' And she struggled to find the word she wanted to convey her meaning. In the absence of a thorough knowledge of theological language she finally said, 'Well, church is such *fun*!'

What did she mean by that? Is our church some kind of comedy club? Have we shelved serious preaching? Are we flippant about sin and irreverent in our worship? Are the members without personal problems? Not at all! I think she noticed the presence of joy in people who are thrilled at their deliverance. So much so that she keeps coming back.

Weapon number 3 – (unity and) community

'The king's decree gave the Jews in every city authority to unite to defend their lives.' (8:11)

'The Jews gathered in their cities throughout all the king's provinces to defend themselves against anyone who might try to harm them. But no one could make a stand against them, for everyone was afraid of them.' (9:2)

Haman's command had gone out to the mass of individuals who weren't Jews, yet Mordecai recognized that this Jewish community needed each other if they were to succeed.

The king's decree gave them the authority they needed to unite. This indicates that they were more scattered up to this point. Perhaps they were restricted by law or intimidated by racism. But now, things were different. They gathered to celebrate, to fight and to rest. They became a powerful force as they rediscovered the strength in their numbers.

Why was everyone afraid of them? Surely it was because they saw God's power displayed in them.

Throughout the Bible God deals initially with individuals, but then promotes community.

In the Old Testament he speaks of Israel, and in the New he focuses on the church as the gathering of believers. In Ephesians 2:19–22 we are described as citizens, his holy people, God's family, his house, a holy temple and joined together as part of the dwelling, where God lives by his spirit.

A godly individual can make an impact on an unbelieving person. Yet you bring a believer into contact with a group of godly individuals then that impact can be immense.

Have you ever felt that in terms of the vast needs in the world that your contribution to meeting them is a bit pathetic? Yet it's predominantly through the *local* group of God's people that God calls us to be active in his service. If every Christian is involved locally the impact nationally and even globally can be so much greater.

Mordecai enabled them to plan and work strategic-ally. They gathered in their own cities to fight. They were mutually encouraged. They celebrated together. They fought together. They rested together.

They gained strength from one another's different gifts. 1 Corinthians 12:12–31 describes the church as a body comprised of many parts working for the good of the whole. Put like that, who wants to be out on a limb when we can be part of a body?

Each contributed to the safety of others looking out for each other as they fought. Where there were weaknesses, others warned and the strong ones filled the gaps.

Community ensured discipline and accountability. No plunder was taken. This leads us on to the next weapon (and blessing) of purity.

Weapon number 4 – purity

The king's edict had given them the same rights as their enemies yet three times in Esther 9, we are told that despite the Jews winning a very great victory over their enemies, they took no plunder. (vv. 10,15,19)

A big deal is made of this so we can be sure that this choice was of huge significance to both God and man. This must have been a community decision, conscien-tiously and clearly made because there are no exceptions throughout the entire empire.

Their purity was a natural response to their deliver-ance. On the day they could have been annihilated, they focused on God-given life and refused to be tain-ted by the habits and possessions of the godless and the dead.

They aligned themselves with the God who had fought for them. They embraced holiness, and his com-mand in 1 Samuel 15, and learnt from the mistakes of history. Way back in the book we looked at the cause of

Haman's hatred. King Saul, rather than completely destroying Haman's ancestors and possessions, kept the best for himself (1 Samuel 15). For this failure and disobedience, he was judged. This time around, God's people were above reproach.

They separated themselves as far as they could from the behaviour of their enemies. They behaved differently from what was expected.

They weren't side-tracked in their battle. They fought, they won, and they gave God the glory due to him. As they celebrated, they concentrated on victory and life rather than possessions.

Their purity and continued deliverance generated generosity and love which fostered community spirit. Rather than examining, comparing and protecting their plunder they gave gifts to one another. This reminds me of some verses in Acts.

> A deep sense of awe came over them all, and the apostles performed many miraculous signs and wonders. And all the believers met together constantly and shared everything they had. They sold their possessions and shared the proceeds with those in need. They worshiped together at the temple each day, met in homes for the Lord's Supper, and shared their meals with great joy and generosity—all the while praising God and enjoying the goodwill of all the people. And each day the Lord added to their group those who were being saved. (2:43–47)

Judgment, visited Persia on 7 and 8 March, 473BC. The total dead in Susa stood at 810. Outside the capital, seventy-five thousand enemies were killed.

Yet it's the miracle of grace that stands out. The grace that spared the Jews was extended to all those outside the nation who came and aligned themselves with them.

Questions for Personal Reflection

1. Read Ephesians 4:11–13. Think through the challenges of being a strong and godly leader. In what areas do these thoughts inspire you to pray for and support your leaders and, if applicable, to develop your own leadership skills?
2. What is at the root of Christian joy? Why is it often so attractive to unbelievers? Why is it often lacking in our lives even as Christians?
3. Read 1 Corinthians 12:12–31. What does this passage tell us about the value God places on individual commitment to the local church? To what extent have you identified and developed your gifts for the good of your fellowship? What are some of the personal blessings commitment to the church bring?
4. How does 2 Corinthians 8:1–15 point to some of the global responsibilities of the local church?
5. Why does Peter stress in 1 Peter 1:13–20 that purity is essential for God's people? Examine the areas of your life that are not marked by holy living.

Permission to Party

☞ *Read ESTHER 9:20–32*

My husband says that I take too long to tell a story. 'Get to the point!' is a common interjection. I argue that because he talks so much generally when I have the floor I need to make the most of it!

I suspect he might be right though. Occasionally in full flow I do detect a flicker of weariness in the eyes of my listener.

In this penultimate chapter of Esther, the narrator uses a lot of words to say a very simple thing. He emphasizes and re-emphasizes the events. It's almost as if he's so excited he can't bear to sign off. The end is as important as what's come before, and unlike my stories that often flop at the conclusion, this climaxes in wonder and anticipation.

Mordecai has a dream

As he enjoys the exhilaration in his heart and witnesses the exuberance of his people Mordecai wants to capture the moment. Not only for his own sake, but so that it can be released to fly to each future generation. He longs that each will be reminded of God's grace, power and deliverance. He desires that every Gentile believer will remember why he or she first believed.

But how could this be done?

A dry history lecture would not suffice, nor a day of serious reflection. Only a party would do. Two days of unabashed revelry and joy. Mordecai is in the business of making memories for people, who so easily forget, and enjoyment is the key. He tells them they need to learn to laugh, and then practice.

I think he's right. I tend to naturally veer towards negativity and misery. Maybe most of us do. I write this at the start of the New Year. And I have to admit I was glad to see the back of the last one. Did anything terrible happen? Not really, but worry got the better of me and I shouldered burdens I was never designed or expected to bear. In actual fact plenty of great things happened too, but I was just too downcast to take much notice.

The thought of preparing for Christmas was almost the last straw. But when it came, I tried to throw myself into it wholeheartedly. Through giving and receiving and making an effort to be cheerful I found my load lifted and I saw what I'd been ignoring for much of the year: the faces of those who love me; and in particular the face of my Saviour Jesus, the light of the world, my deliverer. Celebration had broken the cycle of gloom and as the New Year approached I found I was able to face it with new resolve.

My journal for 2007 opens with these words:

> New Year's resolution: Not to worry. To remember that my shoulders are not built to bear the weight of my troubles or anyone else's. But Christ's are, and I need to be continually unburdening myself onto him. 'Cast all your anxiety on him because he cares for you.' (1 Pet. 5:7, NIV)

Max Lucado writes:

> Where did we get the notion that a good Christian is a
> solemn Christian? Who started the rumour that the sign
> of a disciple is a long face? How did we create this idea
> that the truly gifted are the heavy-hearted?[1]

Maybe you, like me, need to be breaking the cycle of
gloom. Perhaps we, like Mordecai, need to take the time
to make memories and dreams for the future.

A dream based on reality

The dream was possible because it was founded on the
truth. Mordecai didn't want the reason for the season to
be forgotten, or the emphasis for the celebration to shift.
And so he carefully records all the events for future generations.

The reason is summed up in verse 22. 'This would
commemorate a time when the Jews gained relief from
their enemies, when their sorrow was turned into gladness and their mourning into joy.'

This was what had actually happened, but what made
it extra-special and extra-worth remembering is that it
was the reality of the fulfilment of a promise.

Way back in Exodus, another man wrote another
inscription concerning the same issue of the Amalekites.
'Then the LORD instructed Moses, "Write this down as a
permanent record, and announce it to Joshua: I will blot
out every trace of Amalek under heaven."' (Ex. 17:14)

That was the promise. Now God's fulfilled it. It's
done. It's finished. God has been faithful.

The Book of Esther begins and ends with a party. The
first celebrated man's greatness with limitless debauch-
ery, drunkenness, coarseness and obscenity. The second

party focused on God's greatness, and in that they know true, pure and unadulterated gladness, which left no bitter taste in the mouth or tinge of regret.

'Keep it that way!' We almost hear Mordecai say as he turned out his letters. 'Keep your focus, and as you enjoy God, enjoy yourselves!'

True joy *in* and enjoyment *of* God does not need to be a pipe-dream which lasts only as long as a drug-induced high and then disappears like smoke until the next fix.

If we grasp the reality of who God is through his word, his promises and our experiences, we will find this reality will not shift with our moods.

God's dream for us is that we enjoy him. He knows that when we enjoy him we will glorify him.

There are times when we wake up and just feel that contentment in him. At other times of intense difficulty and pain, he will often come to us and simply breathe his joy and peace into us. What about the times in between? Well, he wants us to fight for that joy by grabbing onto the reality of him because it's ours already. Christ died so it could be ours. We might have to fight our way out of the bedclothes to spend that time studying the Bible. We may have to put the ironing aside or turn the radio off in the car so that we can speak to him. Perhaps we need to dust off that journal and write down how God meets us in our daily circumstances. Maybe we need to read back through the events we've already recorded in it and remind ourselves of his faithfulness in the past. Maybe we need to make some replacements: some Christian books for novels, some praise CDs for popular music.

A dream made possible through practicalities

Mordecai went further than simply telling the people to celebrate. He told them how to practically do it.

He told them it was to be an annual event. He told them the dates, the duration and how they were to celebrate. Even the name of the festival had meaning. It was to become a habit that would be almost impossible to break.

'Traditional' has become a dirty word in some Christian circles. It conjures up the image of a depressing style of worship that has remained doggedly unchanged for the last hundred years (or more). And it is seen as culturally irrelevant for the twenty-first century.

Cultural traditions can sometimes strangle the life out of us, but biblical ones when properly practised give and foster life. You just can't beat them! The New Testament is full of them.

Look at these and note how positive they are:

> And let us not neglect our meeting together, as some people do, but encourage and warn each other, especially now that the day of his coming back again is drawing near. (Heb. 10:25)

> On the night when he was betrayed, the Lord Jesus took a loaf of bread, and when he had given thanks, he broke it and said, "This is my body, which is given for you. Do this in remembrance of me." In the same way, he took the cup of wine after supper, saying, "This cup is the new covenant between God and you, sealed by the shedding of my blood. Do this in remembrance of me as often as you drink it." For every time you eat this bread and drink this cup, you are announcing the Lord's death until he comes again. (1 Cor. 11:23b–26)

> Keep on praying. (1 Thes. 5:17)

> Let the words of Christ, in all their richness, live in your hearts and make you wise. Use his words to teach and counsel each other. (Col. 3:16)

> So don't worry about tomorrow, for tomorrow will bring its own worries. (Mt 6:34a)

And remember this one?

> 'Always be full of joy in the Lord. I say it again – rejoice!' (Phil. 4:4)

What is the aim of these commands? A life filled with the enjoyment of God! These principles are to become practised until they become habits we can't live without. My gym instructor says, 'Exercise should be a way of life.' Going to the gym isn't a problem for me when I'm in a routine. But when that routine is broken because of illness or a couple of busy weeks, then boy do I find it hard to get back into the swing of it.

Biblical traditions need to be a way of life. Here are some of the ones I've tried to hold to, some for years, others more recently.

- When God's people are meeting, I should be there with them unless I have a very good reason not to.
- I should take practical steps to stop the progression of anxious thoughts before they spiral out of control, concentrating instead on the promises of God to provide.
- I should make a conscious effort to list the things to praise God for and replace my moans and groans with them.
- My days and weeks need to be ordered in such a way that there are regular opportunities for reading his

word and prayer and worship, recognizing that when I don't have a routine my personal times with the Lord are often the first to go.

When it comes to personal devotions, I was brought up on the advice that the same time and the same place helps in terms of a consistent walk. That might sound old-fashioned – but if it keeps me focused on God, does it matter? Admittedly most of us find there are seasons of our lives when that's not always easy or even possible such as in times of bereavement, relationship break-downs, illness, mad exam times or when caring for young, elderly or sick relatives. At those times I try to remind myself that God understands. He's a God of grace and love, not a tyrant with a big stick. I was grate-ful to the thoughtful friend who wrote Isaiah 40:11 in a card when my daughter was born:

> He will feed his flock like a shepherd. He will carry the lambs in his arms, holding them close to his heart. He will gently lead the mother sheep with their young.

Elizabeth Prentiss, the American nineteenth-century author, understood this. She wrote:

> One of the hard things about bereavement is the physical prostration and listlessness which makes it next to impossible to pray, and quite impossible to feel the least interest in anything . . . We must bear this as part of the pain, believing that it will not last for ever.

Elsewhere she stated:

> I used to reproach myself for religious stupidity when not well, but see now that God is my kind Father – not

my hard task master, expecting me to be full of life and zeal when physically exhausted. It takes long to learn such lessons.[2]

On the whole, routines are reassuring. Seven days in a week, 24 hours in a day, the rise and fall of the tide, regular mealtimes around the table, another Christmas, another birthday, the bus that keeps to its timetable. Sometimes, though, that same routine, however pleasant, can become boring and predictable. Christian living isn't meant to be marked by burdensome regulation but with fresh joy and celebration.

Mordecai safeguards this celebration from becoming a routine in a rut by decreeing that the time should be marked with generosity. Not only to family and friends but also to the poor. They are to step out of their comfort zone and acknowledge others. As they do this, they will both be reminded of and mirror God's generosity to them.

A dream shared (vv. 29–32)

Just when we think he and everyone in Persia have got the idea, Esther writes a letter. In fact, she writes several letters. The first was filled with authority, and others sent greetings and reassurance. These letters established Purim.

Mordecai delivered the idea, Esther made it happen. The suggestion is that Mordecai couldn't do this alone. He needed her.

I ask myself how I'm perceived in my family and church. Am I known as a woman who is predictably negative? Do I undermine others enthusiasm with cynicism? Do I spoil new initiatives by putting up hurdles of antagonism and criticism? Do I distance myself in case of failure?

Am I only enthusiastic about my own ideas? Or, like Esther do I share the dreams of others and then seek to enhance and enforce them by my support and enthusiasm?

There are some strident women who are vocal and opinionated and do their best to spoil good ideas in churches and families alike. (Especially if the idea is from a man!) Esther truly wanted the best for God's people, and did all she could to achieve that. She took her position seriously.

After her death, Tony Blair called Princess Diana 'The People's Princess.' She was said to have the common touch. Despite her position and beauty, she literally reached out to the needy, and she was perceived as one who cared. She was loved in return. Esther took this principle several stages further. She wasn't only concerned for the physical and emotional welfare, but also the spiritual good of her people. Not only did she seek to touch those in her day, but also every generation she would never see. She had a big heart and was in the true sense of the word, 'The People's Queen.'

A dream caught

Without the united determination of the people it's unlikely that the idea would have worked so effectively. It's still practised today among the Jews.

Michele Guinness is a second-generation British Jew and became a Christian as a schoolgirl. She writes vividly of Purim in her autobiography, *Child of the Covenant*:

> Mother only insisted we attend the synagogue on major festivals, but since she rarely came with us, even that seemed a bit much at times. One festival was too good to be missed however – *Purim*, the Feast of Esther. The

synagogue was quite noisy on most occasions, with people coming and going and kissing their relatives as they came or went, but the rabbi only stopped the service when he could no longer hear what he was saying himself. He would rest his elbows on the pulpit and, tapping his foot with a look of mock weariness on his face, stare at the women's gallery where most of the noise was coming from, until the realisation dawned that the service had come to a standstill and a temporary, penitent silence would descend. But at *Purim* the more noise the better. As the rabbi recounted the famous story of Esther, we booed with all our might every time the name Haman was mentioned, and cheered loudly for Esther and Mordecai.[3]

The Jews love the idea, why? '. . . because of Mordecai's letter and because of what they'd experienced.' (v. 26). What a great verse that is!

Firstly, they respected Mordecai. They loved him because he loved them. His love was proven, they accepted that he knew and wanted the best, and what he said made sense. It was for their good.

1 John 4:19 reads, 'We love because he first loved us.' (NIV)

Similarly, my love for God and others is a response to the realisation of the indisputable fact that God loves me even though I never did anything to deserve that love.

Secondly, they again focused on their deliverance. They wanted to hold on to the reality of that.

Their love for God's people had extended to generations as yet unknown. Celebration was a joy, not a burden.

John's letter continues 'This is how we know that we love the children of God: by loving God and carrying out his commands. This is love for God: to obey his

commands. And his commands are not burdensome'
(1 Jn. 5:2–3, NIV).

If I remember God's love, then I recognize his best for others and for me. Obedience is then a delight. Yet when I forget his love, that obedience becomes a burden. I feel I'm missing out on something better. I become selfish and rebellious.

I remember as a child being taught: God is more interested in our holiness than our happiness

I agree. Up to a point. But why do we always talk as if it's an either/or situation? Actually I think he is very interested in our happiness but knows that it comes hand-in-hand with holiness.

God has given us the church, so we might inspire one another with a united response and a catching of the dream of remembrance and celebration, proven by obedience and generosity of spirit.

The apostle John went on to have a vision of his own.

> After this I saw a vast crowd, too great to count, from every nation and tribe and people and language, standing in front of the throne and before the Lamb. They were clothed in white and held palm branches in their hands. And they were shouting with a mighty shout, "Salvation comes from our God on the throne and from the Lamb!" (Rev. 7:9–10)

Have you caught this dream? Are our churches gripped in expectancy in our singing and Sunday worship? Are we marked with generosity? Are we reaching out to those nations and tribes and people who we'll spend eternity with? Are we gathering them in? Are we welcoming them in? Are we planning for the future generations of the church? Are we equipping our children and new Christians? Are we discipling and mentoring?

Perhaps the Jews, like me, veered naturally towards seriousness. They'd already set aside times of fasting and mourning (v. 31), and we have to admire them for this.

But Mordecai and Esther gave them the permission to lighten up.

To enjoy God.

To enjoy themselves.

What a relief!

Questions for Personal Reflection

1. What are the biblical routines you need to establish in your life and how can they enhance joy?
2. John Piper writes, 'If a man can rob you of your joy he can rob you of your usefulness.'[4] What do you think he means by that? Do you agree?
3. In Philippians 4 what are some of the keys Paul gives to promoting and maintaining Christian joy?
4. Many Christians are plagued with clinical depression and most suffer times of deep discouragement. There is convincing evidence in the Psalms that King David shared that suffering (Psalm 42 is just one such example). Read Lamentations 3:16–33. What assurances are we given in times when the feelings of joy have deserted us?

11

All for Good

☞ *Read ESTHER 10*

It can be fun inventing epitaphs for those we know. How would we sum up their lives in just a few words? My grandmother died last year. At the funeral, a friend described her as 'a good egg.' I loved that. Despite my tears, I laughed out loud. It encapsulated everything about her – her generosity, her godliness, her sense of fun and her wisdom.

A friend some years ago was nicknamed Earnest by some other friends I think he suspected of teasing him. Perhaps they were but actually 'He was earnest' would be the most fitting epitaph for him. He continues to be very earnest in his ministry, his family life, and his walk with God in a way that always challenges me.

In the last three verses of Esther, we're left with enough information to create epitaphs for two powerful men.

One might read:

**HERE LIES XERXES – BUILDER OF HIS OWN
GREAT EMPIRE**

The other:

HERE LIES MORDECAI – BUILDER OF GOD'S ETERNAL KINGDOM

Mordecai continued to work for the good of God's people. He never forgot his roots, or his first love. He never separated himself from the Jews, and despite his greatness and authority was still called their friend.

In some ways, nothing had changed. Xerxes still ruled. The Persian Empire still dominated. They were still far from their homeland. Their cause still needed championing and their welfare wasn't an automatic consideration.

But in other ways, everything had changed. This was a different people to those we met at the beginning of this book. Not long after the Jews were taken into captivity God gave Jeremiah a vision of good and bad figs placed before the temple followed with this message:

> The good figs represent the exiles I sent from Judah to the land of the Babylonians. I have sent them into captivity for their own good. I will see that they are well treated, and I will bring them back here again. I will build them up and not tear them down. I will plant them and not uproot them. I will give them hearts that will recognize me as the Lord. They will be my people, and I will be their God, for they will return to me wholeheartedly. (Jer. 24:5b–7)

They were changed. The Babylonians meant to harm them. But God had meant it for good. Haman had meant to annihilate them, but God again meant it for good. Their faith had become stronger through the survival of despair. God was building them up for their 'whole-hearted' return home. He had provided them with Esther and Mordecai to ensure his promise that they would be well treated would be met. With Mordecai pleading their case before the king's throne they were safe, and they enjoyed some years of stability.

What qualified Mordecai for this job as intercessor between the king and the Jews?

- The king trusted him.
- The king had given him authority.
- He knew his people. He walked where they walked. He felt their pain and understood their struggles. He recognized their needs.
- His love for them was proven. The Jews trusted him for all he'd done and continued to do for them.

Wouldn't it be great to have someone like Mordecai fighting for Christians in Parliament? It's right to pray that God would raise up such leaders and to pray for those who lead already. Yet human governments are only temporary. King Xerxes, for all his greatness, was a mere man. Ten years after the events recorded in Esther, he was assassinated. His son, Artexerxes, succeeded him, and we hear no more of Mordecai or Queen Esther. Eventually the empire even crumbled. But God is still on the throne.

No one can topple him. No one can obstruct his promises or divert his purposes. Both can be traced through the remaining pages of Scripture. We watch as he manages the Jews return home with the permission of Artexerxes, and the leadership of Nehemiah.

We celebrate the coming of Christ, the hope of Jew and Gentile alike. We learn from his life and mourn his death. We rejoice at his resurrection and feel the loss of his return heavenward. We are comforted by the Holy Spirit and now long for his return, prophesied but as yet unfulfilled.

And as we wait . . . we remember that someone even greater than Mordecai intercedes and pleads for us before God's eternal and all-powerful throne.

Hebrews 4:14–16 explains:

> That is why we have a great High Priest who has gone to heaven, Jesus the Son of God. Let us cling to him and never stopped trusting him. This High Priest of ours understands our weaknesses, for he faced all of the same temptations we do, yet he did not sin. So let us come boldly to the throne of our gracious God. There we will receive his mercy, and we will find grace to help us when we need it.

What qualifies Christ to do this for us?

1. He's divine. He's the Son of God (v. 14), not merely the Prime Minister.
2. God trusts him because of his obedience. Hebrews 5:8 tells us that, 'So even though Jesus was God's son, he learned obedience from the things he suffered.'
3. His love for us is proven through that suffering.
4. His Father gave him the authority to do this job. Hebrews 5:9 states 'God qualified him as a perfect High Priest.'
5. He empathizes because he's walked where we walk. He has gone through everything we go through. He knows how we feel. He knows what we need through experience.
6. He is sinless. He is genuinely better than us.
7. He doesn't just plead for us, but gives us access to the throne of his father. His presence permits us to be brave and bold and guarantees our safety.
8. His position is permanent.

9. God is gracious and we are promised everything we need. There are no exceptions. He's predictably good. He won't be generous one day and fly off the handle the next.

For all these reasons 'Let us cling to him and never stop trusting him' (Heb. 4:14b) makes perfect sense. Christ is a true friend.

John MacArthur in his commentary on Matthew's Gospel notes:

> Some believers suffer more than others, but all suffer at some time and in some way. In spite of that, the storm is never so severe, the night never so black, and the boat never so frail that we risk danger beyond our Father's care.[1]

We know our troubles will never be over, as long as we remain on this fallen earth. None of us can predict what lies ahead. But God knows, and just as God promised the Jews that their exile experiences would be for their good. So we are to be assured, 'that God causes everything to work together for the good of those who love God and are called according to his purpose for them.' (Rom. 8:28)

Humanly speaking Ronald Dunn seems to have had more than his fair share of suffering including the suicide of his son. Yet on this verse he writes 'If this is true, it means that if God subtracted one pain, one heartache, one disappointment from my life, I would be less than the person God wants me to be, and my ministry would be less than He intends.'[2]

We're going home. He's just getting us ready.

Questions for Personal Reflection

1. How would you like your epitaph to read? Realistically, if you died today, how would others remember you?
2. What does 1 Corinthians 3:6–17 teach us about our personal responsibilities regarding the building of God's kingdom?
3. Why is Hebrews 4:14–16 such an encouragement as we struggle with our weaknesses?
4. Consider Romans 8:18–39. Take time to praise God for his hand on your life and the promises for the present and the future.

Appendix

Who Were the Eunuchs?

Eunuchs were males who had been castrated. This wilful mutilation violated God's creation plan. So serious was the offence and to deter the practice they were not allowed into the assembly of the Lord (Deut. 23:1; 25:11).

Eunuchs originally had no place in Jewish society and were associated with pagan practices. The first incident of eunuchs appearing in Israel is in the court of Ahab and pagan Jezebel (2 Kgs. 9:30–37).

Pagan parents used to castrate their sons, so they could serve in the houses of the great. Traditionally, they were considered sexually safe and ideal keepers of the harem (although some dispute that). The Greek words 'eune' and 'ekheih' literally mean 'bed-keeper'.

They were also regarded as a politically safe because their inability to produce offspring reduced their political ambition. Their appearance was distinctive: their shape curvy; their skin smooth; and they tended to live longer than other males. But throughout the story of Esther these 'symbols of disgrace' in Israel play a major role.

God's mercy was extended to Esther and her people through these unlikely sources. And God extended his grace to them.

And my blessings are for Gentiles, too, when they commit themselves to the LORD. Do not let them think that I consider them second-class citizens. And my blessings are also for the eunuchs. They are as much mine as anyone else. For I say this to the eunuchs who keep my Sabbath days holy, who choose to do what pleases me and commit their lives to me: I will give them – in my house, within my walls – a memorial and a name far greater than the honor they would have received by having sons and daughters. For the name I give them is an everlasting one. It will never disappear! (Is. 56:3–5)

In Acts 8:26–38 we read of an Ethiopian eunuch realising that Christ came and died for him. We witness both his conversion and his baptism. This story illustrates God's grace beautifully, as, I hope you have discovered, does the Book of Esther.

Endnotes

Introduction

[1] Johanna-Ruth Dobschiner, *Selected to Live* (London: Pickering & Inglis, 1974).

Chapter 1

[1] Charles Swindoll, *Esther* (Nashville: Word Publishing, 1997).
[2] Alexander Strauch, *Men and Women, Equal Yet Different* (Missouri: College Press Publishing, 1999).
[3] John Piper, *What's the Difference?* (Wheaton: Crossway Books, 1990).
[4] Swindoll, *Esther.*

Chapter 2

[1] Tony Payne and Phillip D. Jensen, *Pure Sex* (New Malden: Matthias Media, 1998).
[2] *OK!* 30 Jan 2007, issue 556.
[3] Tom Holland, *Persian Fire* (London: Little, Brown, 2005).
[4] Ceefax Files, *10 Things We Didn't Know Last Week* (15 April 2006).

5 Linda Dillow and Lorraine Pintus, *Intimate Issues: 21 Questions Christian Women Ask about Sex* (Eastbourne: Kingsway Publications, 1999).

6 Corrie Ten Boom, *The Hiding Place* (London: Hodder & Stoughton, 2004).

7 © J. Carswell, *Interview between Helen Roseveare and Jonathan Carswell* (19 Feb 2007).

Chapter 3

1 Don Stephens, *War and Grace* (Darlington: Evangelical Press, 2005).

2 Diet Eman with James Schapp, *Things we Couldn't Say* (Oxford: Monarch Books, 2005).

3 Samuel Rutherford, source unknown.

4 Joseph Hart, 'How Good is the God We Adore', as quoted in *Christian Hymns* (Bridgend: Evangelical Movement of Wales, 1977).

Chapter 4

1 John White, *The Fight* (Downers Grove: Inter–Varsity Press, 1987).

2 Linda Dillow, *Calm my Anxious Heart* (Colorado Springs: NavPress, 1998).

3 Michele Guinness, *Child of the Covenant* (London: Hodder & Stoughton, 2005).

4 White, *The Fight*.

5 Della Thompson (ed.) *The Oxford Compact English Dictionary* (Oxford: Oxford University Press, 1996).

6 The information in this paragraph and the 'Power' bullet point is taken from Holland, *Persian Fire*.

7 White, *The Fight*.

[8] C. S. Lewis, *Mere Christianity* (London: HarperCollins, 1997).
[9] Elisabeth Elliot, *The Mark of a Man* (London: Hodder & Stoughton, 1981).

Chapter 5

[1] Charles Swindoll, *Living Above the Level of Mediocrity* (Nashville: Word Publishing, 1989).
[2] James Dobson, *Man to Man About Women* (Eastbourne: Kingsway Publications, 1984).
[3] dc Talk & The Voice of the Martyrs, *Jesus Freaks* (Guildford: Eagle Publishing, 2000).
[4] Horatio Gates Spafford, 'When Peace Like A River' as quoted in *Christian Hymns*.
[5] Dillow, *Calm my Anxious Heart*.

Chapter 6

[1] Thompson, *The Oxford Compact English Dictionary*.
[2] John Pollock, *D.L. Moody* (Fearne: Christian Focus, 2005).
[3] Swindoll, *Living Above the Level of Mediocrity*.
[4] Darlene Deibler Rose, *Evidence Not Seen* (Carlisle: Authentic Lifestyle, 2002).
[5] Eareckson, Joni, *Joni* (Edinburgh: Pickering & Inglis, 1982).

Chapter 7

[1] Charles Spurgeon, *Satan: A Defeated Foe* (New Kensington: Whitaker House, 1993).
[2] William Cowper, 'What Various Hindrances We Meet' as quoted in *Christian Hymns*.
[3] Spurgeon, *Satan: A Defeated Foe*.

Chapter 8

[1] Mary Soames, *Clementine Churchill* (London: Penguin Books, 1981).

[2] Thompson, *The Oxford Compact English Dictionary.*

Chapter 9

[1] Spurgeon, *Satan: A Defeated Foe.*

[2] Ronald Dunn, *When Heaven is Silent* (Nashville: Word Publishing, 1994).

[3] Swindoll, *Living Above the Level of Mediocrity.*

[4] Martin Luther, source unknown.

Chapter 10

[1] Max Lucado, *When God Whispers Your Name* (Nashville: Word Publishing, 1994).

[2] Sharon James, *Elizabeth Prentiss* (Edinburgh: The Banner of Truth Trust, 2006).

[3] Guinness, *Child of the Covenant.*

[4] John Piper, *Amazing Grace in the Life of William Wilberforce* (Downers Grove: Inter-Varsity Press, 2007).

Chapter 11

[1] John MacArthur, *The MacArthur New Testament Commentary: Matthew 8–15* (Chicago: Moody Bible Institute, 1987).

[2] Ronald Dunn, *When Heaven is Silent* (Nashville: Word Publishing, 1994).

Bibliography

Unless otherwise referenced, all Bible quotations are from the New Living Translation.

Alexander, Hilary, 24 May 2006, www.telegraph.co.uk.

MacArthur, John, *The MacArthur Study Bible* (Nashville: Word Publishing, 1987).

Acknowledgements

Special thanks to:

Wes, Caitlin and Caleb. Thank you for the many sacrifices you've made to make this book possible.

Mum and Dad for patiently taking countless phone calls when I've been discouraged.

Brenda Scott for cheerfully interpreting my scrawl and getting everything onto disk.

Charlotte Hubback for your sensitive editing and helpful comments over the last year.

Mark Finnie and Jonathan Carswell who gave me the opportunity to write.

The Slade Church Family and everyone who has prayed for me and encouraged me along the way.

And most of all . . . *my Heavenly Father.* Thank you for opening my eyes to some of the amazing truths and promises contained in Esther's story and for making those treasures mine.